T0311450

Cambridge Elements

Elements in Politics and Communication
edited by
Stuart Soroka
University of California

HOW NEWS COVERAGE OF MISINFORMATION SHAPES PERCEPTIONS AND TRUST

Emily Thorson
Syracuse University

CAMBRIDGE
UNIVERSITY PRESS

CAMBRIDGE
UNIVERSITY PRESS

Shaftesbury Road, Cambridge CB2 8EA, United Kingdom

One Liberty Plaza, 20th Floor, New York, NY 10006, USA

477 Williamstown Road, Port Melbourne, VIC 3207, Australia

314–321, 3rd Floor, Plot 3, Splendor Forum, Jasola District Centre,
New Delhi – 110025, India

103 Penang Road, #05–06/07, Visioncrest Commercial, Singapore 238467

Cambridge University Press is part of Cambridge University Press & Assessment,
a department of the University of Cambridge.

We share the University's mission to contribute to society through the pursuit of
education, learning and research at the highest international levels of excellence.

www.cambridge.org
Information on this title: www.cambridge.org/9781009488846

DOI: 10.1017/9781009488815

© Emily Thorson 2024

This publication is in copyright. Subject to statutory exception and to the provisions
of relevant collective licensing agreements, no reproduction of any part may take
place without the written permission of Cambridge University Press & Assessment.

When citing this work, please include a reference to the DOI 10.1017/9781009488815

First published 2024

A catalogue record for this publication is available from the British Library.

ISBN 978-1-009-48884-6 Hardback
ISBN 978-1-009-48880-8 Paperback
ISSN 2633-9897 (online)
ISSN 2633-9889 (print)

Additional resources for this publication at www.cambridge.org/9781009488846

Cambridge University Press & Assessment has no responsibility for the persistence
or accuracy of URLs for external or third-party internet websites referred to in this
publication and does not guarantee that any content on such websites is, or will
remain, accurate or appropriate.

How News Coverage of Misinformation Shapes Perceptions and Trust

Elements in Politics and Communication

DOI: 10.1017/9781009488815
First published online: May 2024

Emily Thorson
Syracuse University

Author for correspondence: Emily Thorson, ethorson@gmail.com

Abstract: This Element takes on two related questions: How do the media cover the issue of misinformation, and how does exposure to this coverage affect public perceptions, including trust? A content analysis shows that most media coverage explicitly blames social media for the problem, and two experiments find that while exposure to news coverage of misinformation makes people less trusting of news on social media, it increases trust in print news. This counterintuitive effect occurs because exposure to news about misinformation increases the perceived value of traditional journalistic norms. Finally, exposure to misinformation coverage has no measurable effect on political trust or internal efficacy, and political interest is a strong predictor of interest in news coverage of misinformation across partisan lines. These results suggest that many Americans see legacy media as a bulwark against changes that threaten to distort the information environment.

Keywords: misinformation, fake news, media coverage, agenda-setting, media trust

© Emily Thorson 2024

ISBNs: 9781009488846 (HB), 9781009488808 (PB), 9781009488815 (OC)
ISSNs: 2633-9897 (online), 2633-9889 (print)

Contents

1 Introduction

While misinformation has always been a part of the media ecosystem, the 2016 election was an inflection point for its prominence in public discourse. A 2017 *Time* magazine cover asked, in stark red letters, "Is Truth Dead?" A 2016 *Economist* cover heralded the advent of "Post-truth politics in the age of social media." News magazines were not the only ones paying attention. In the wake of the election, "post-truth," "misinformation," and "fake news" were each named "word of the year" by (respectively) the Oxford Dictionaries, Dictionary.com, and Collins Dictionary (Funke 2018*a*). Local and national news outlets reported on these decisions, and in doing so called even more attention to the issue of misinformation (Diaz 2018; Italie 2018; Strauss 2018). Wrote Emily Jacobs at the *New York Post*, "the word-of-the-year decision comes as social media companies, and the American people, grapple with the now-global struggle surrounding 'fake news'" (Jacobs 2018). The often hyperbolic media attention garnered by these (relatively inconsequential) "word of the year" decisions aptly illustrates the mainstream media's earnest attention to the phenomenon of misinformation (Tsfati et al. 2020).

Despite these initial concerns that exposure to misinformation was widespread, empirical assessments have consistently shown a pattern of low average exposure. For most people, misinformation is a tiny fraction of their information diet (Guess, Nagler and Tucker 2019): for example, Allen et al. (2020) find that "fake news" comprises just 0.15% of Americans' daily media exposure. But while many Americans may have relatively little *direct* experience with misinformation, the intense media coverage of the issue likely provides them with a great deal of *indirect* experience, painting the "pictures in their heads" that shape not only how they conceive of the problem, but also who they hold responsible for it (Lippmann 1922; Iyengar 1994).

This Elements investigates how media coverage of the misinformation phenomenon shapes public beliefs and attitudes, including media trust. I show that exposure to news coverage of misinformation has the surprising effect of *increasing* trust in mainstream media, and in particular print news. Drawing on data from a content analysis and three experiments, I argue that this unexpected pattern is a direct result of how the media frame responsibility for misinformation: as largely the fault of social media. News coverage of misinformation paints a picture of often-toxic social media platforms where anyone can post "fake news" and gatekeeping is nonexistent. This coverage shapes Americans' beliefs not only about who is to blame for misinformation, but also who can best protect them against it. Print media – with its professional standards and commitment to checking sources – is perceived as a bulwark against the post-truth chaos of social media.

1.1 The News Media's Fascination with Misinformation

Journalists see misinformation and "fake news" as an especially serious problem partly because it has the potential to directly undermine their work, and these concerns in turn inform the nature of their coverage. A 2022 Pew survey of working journalists shows that they are even more concerned than the American public about made-up news: 71% of journalists say it is a "very big problem," compared to 50% of the public (Gottfried et al. 2022). In addition, 58% report having had conversations with colleagues about misinformation at least several times a month over the past year.

Journalists' concern over misinformation is not only a topic of water-cooler conversation – it has also inspired a number of conferences focused on strategies for both combatting and covering "fake news." For example, in 2019, the American Press Institute convened "Truth-Telling in the Modern Age: Strategies to Confront Polarization and Misinformation" with representatives from media institutions both local (e.g. the *Knoxville News Sentinel*, the *Boston Globe*) and national (e.g. *The New York Times* and *The Washington Post*). In 2021, the Shorenstein Center at Harvard hosted a "News Leaders Summit" with participants from outlets ranging from CNN and the Associated Press to Buzzfeed and *The Atlantic*, with the stated goal of "bring[ing] together small cohorts of news and media leaders to tackle the problem of misinformation-at-scale and media manipulation within the industry." Also in 2021, the BBC hosted a conference entitled "Trust in News: The View from the Frontline Fighting Disinformation," featuring speakers from Reuters, the Canadian Broadcasting Corporation (CBC), and Facebook. While conferences that bring together journalists to talk about an emerging issue can be both helpful and informative, it is worth noting the unusual amount of attention paid to misinformation in particular, especially compared to other novel issues that have emerged over the last decade.

Why is misinformation of such intense concern to journalists, especially given social science research suggesting that absolute levels of public exposure to "fake news" are relatively low (Allen et al. 2020; Guess, Nyhan and Reifler 2020)? There are several potential explanations. First, misinformation runs counter to one of the core normative commitments of journalism: to ensure a functioning democracy by creating an informed public. To the extent that misinformation has the ability to change behavior or attitudes (including vote choice), it has the potential to threaten democracy. As Richard Hasen put it in *The New York Times*, "False information about Covid-19 vaccines meant to undermine confidence in government or the Biden presidency has had deadly consequences" (Hasen 2022). While these concerns are real, they may also be heightened by journalists' own self-identity and perception of their roles. Analyzing at how journalists covered misinformation during November of 2016, Carlson (2020) characterizes their response as an "informational moral panic" in which they "cast fake news as polluting the information environment, sowing confusion, and undermining legitimate news."

Of course, the "fake news" headlines circulating on social media (e.g. "Pope Endorses Donald Trump") are just one type of misinformation. Another critical, and arguably more influential, source of false claims is political elites. During the 2020 election, former President Donald Trump's false claims about election fraud had measurable impacts on public trust in elections (Berlinski et al. 2023). When deciding how to cover claims like these, journalists are faced with several difficult choices. First, there is the choice of whether to cover these false claims at all. On the one hand, reporting on elite statements is part of their mission. On the other hand, repeating false claims – even if only to correct them – has the potential consequence of ensuring that they reach a broader audience than they would otherwise (Tsfati et al. 2020). McClure Haughey et al. (2020) note this tension in interviews with journalists on the "misinformation beat," describing their struggle to "[weigh] the risk of amplifying a marginal and problematic narrative into the mainstream against the danger of ignoring it."

Then, even if they do decide to repeat the false claims, they face the choice of how to cover them: by correcting them directly (i.e. using their authority to explicitly state that the claim is false, sometimes referred to as "journalistic arbitration") or by offering a competing perspective (i.e. quoting a different politician making a competing claim; sometimes referred to as the "he-said, she-said" approach). Each of these approaches comes with both costs and benefits. While journalistic arbitration can be more effective at reducing belief in misinformation (Thorson 2018), it also has the potential to threaten a news source's credibility if a reader sees this arbitration as evidence of political bias (Shin 2023).

Journalists' concerns over misinformation are thus multifaceted. First, they worry that exposure to misinformation may threaten democratic functioning by creating a misinformed public. Second, they perceive that the act of correcting misinformation may also erode trust: because elites are a major source of false claims, journalists are faced with the thorny problem of how to accurately cover these false claims while also avoiding accusations of bias. Finally, the use of "fake news" as a rhetorical strategy deliberately wielded to undermine journalistic authority poses a more existential threat. Given this constellation of ethical and practical worries that directly affect their livelihood and identity, it is perhaps unsurprising that journalists are uniquely attentive to the problems of misinformation – and that this attention may influence both the volume and nature of their coverage.

In addition, as technological changes facilitate new entrants to the media marketplace (including both social media and niche partisan outlets), journalists are faced with increasing pressure to capture audience attention (Munger 2020; Nelson 2021). If coverage of "fake news" is particularly compelling to potential readers (as measured in clicks, views, or engagement), then journalists may feel pressured to cover the topic even in spite of ethical qualms.

1.2 Public Perceptions of Misinformation and "Fake News"

This Element takes on two related questions: How do the media cover misinformation, and what effects does this coverage have on the public's beliefs and attitudes? While the previous section lays out some of the factors that may shape journalists' conceptions of "fake news" and misinformation, this section discusses how the public views these phenomena.

Just as media attention to misinformation has grown over the last decade, so has the issue's perceived importance among the public. And indeed, many people are both deeply concerned about misinformation and convinced that it is omnipresent. Americans estimate that about 39% of the news in TV, newspaper, and radio is misinformation, along with 65% of the news on social media (Gallup 2018). Two-thirds say that made-up news has caused "a great deal of confusion" about the basic facts of current events (Barthel, Mitchell and Holcomb 2016). In a cross-national survey, 64% of Americans reported that they were very or extremely concerned about "what is real and what is fake on the internet when it comes to news," substantially more than the average (54%) across the twenty-five countries surveyed (Newman 2018). Among the 64% of Americans who think that social media has a "mostly negative" effect on the way things are going in the United States today, a plurality cite misinformation and made-up news as the primary reason (Auxier 2020).

The tandem rise of media attention to and public concern over misinformation is consistent with a long literature showing the agenda-setting power of media: from issues ranging from the environment to crime, the more the media covers an issue, the more people see it as important (McCombs and Shaw 1972; McCombs 2005). However, the association alone is not sufficient to show that media coverage of the topic has influenced public opinion. A plausible alternate explanation is that *direct* exposure to misinformation has led people to see it as a problem. If people are regularly encountering misinformation in their day-to-day life, they may come to see it as a major threat.

At the same time that concern about misinformation has risen, trust in media – and political trust more broadly – has declined. Since 1972, Gallup has asked, "In general, how much trust and confidence do you have in the mass media – such as newspapers, TV and radio – when it comes to reporting the news fully, accurately and fairly?" In the 1970s, around 70% of people reported that they trusted the mass media a great deal or a fair amount. By 2022, this number had fallen to just 22%, with the decline largely concentrated among Republicans (Brenan 2022).

The fact that as self-reported exposure to misinformation has increased, trust in media has decreased is not in and of itself evidence of a causal relationship between the two. However, many scholars have raised concerns that either direct or indirect exposure to misinformation might have effects beyond simply belief in false claims. A 2018 assessment of the dangers of misinformation published in *Science* warns that "[b]eyond electoral impacts, what we know about the effects of media more generally suggests many potential pathways of influence, from increasing cynicism and apathy to encouraging extremism" (Lazer et al. 2018). Tsfati et al. (2020) emphasize that "many people may hear about fake news stories through mainstream news media," and point to the need for experimental research examining the effects of this coverage not only on belief, but also on related attitudes such as media trust.

In addition, there are several reasons to believe that Democrats and Republicans may respond differently to news coverage of misinformation. Substantial research shows that there is a large partisan asymmetry in misinformation in the information ecosystem. Statements made by Republican politicians are more likely than their Democratic counterparts to be found "false" by fact-checkers (Ferracioli, Kniess and Marques 2022), Republicans are more likely than Democrats to visit "fake news" websites (Guess, Nyhan and Reifler 2020), and conservatives see more misinformation on Facebook than liberals (González-Bailón et al. 2023). In addition, starting in 2016, then-candidate Donald Trump began using the term "fake news" as a catch-all critique of any news coverage with which he disagreed, and this rhetoric may differentially shape how Republicans respond to either misinformation or coverage of the phenomenon (Van Duyn and Collier 2018; Farhall et al. 2019). Given these concerns, as well as the discrepancy in media trust between Democrats and Republicans, throughout this Element I explore partisan differences in responses to news coverage of misinformation.

1.3 Overview of Studies

This Element explores the nature and effects of media coverage of misinformation using a multi-method approach. First, a content analysis analyzes more than 800 articles about the misinformation phenomenon published in four major media outlets. These articles all explicitly explore the issue of misinformation, with headlines like "How Do We Get to Herd Immunity for Fake News?" and "YouTube Bans All Anti-Vaccine Misinformation." The content analysis shows not only that news headlines focused on the misinformation phenomenon have increased over the past eight years, but also that in these articles, journalists overwhelmingly characterize misinformation as a problem endemic to *social* media (e.g. Facebook and Twitter).

Next, I draw on existing theory to formulate hypotheses about how exposure to misinformation coverage might impact beliefs about the prevalence of misinformation as well as media and political trust. I also present the results of a pretest examining potential partisan differences in perceptions of this coverage. In the pretest, participants are asked to evaluate whether twenty headlines (including eight about misinformation, all based on real headlines) are biased against Democrats, Republicans, or neither. The pretest yields two major findings: neither Republicans nor Democrats perceive news coverage of misinformation as having more partisan bias than political coverage more generally, and the term "fake news" does not elicit more perceptions of partisan bias than the term "misinformation."

Both the pretest and the content analysis directly inform two survey experiments. In the first, participants are randomly assigned to view a series of headlines about either misinformation, or elections, or to a pure control condition. I find that exposure to the headlines about misinformation (e.g. "Google Announces Plan to Combat Spread of Fake News") has no effect on political trust, but increases trust in media. The second experiment replicates and extends that finding, showing that making news coverage of misinformation more salient increases trust in print media, and decreases trust in social media. Finally, a third exploratory study offers an explanation for this counterintuitive effect on media trust: exposure to news about misinformation increases the salience of professional journalistic norms such as relying on credible sources and validating facts, and reduces concerns about biased coverage.

2 Media Attention to the Misinformation Phenomenon

While substantial research has tracked the rise of journalistic fact-checking initiatives designed to debunk specific falsehoods (Graves 2016; Graves, Nyhan and Reifler 2016; Amazeen 2020), we have fewer systematic investigations of how the media have covered the larger phenomenon of misinformation and "fake news." This section briefly summarizes some of the existing work looking at journalistic responses to misinformation.

Carlson (2020) examines how the media coverage of "fake news" in November of 2016, the month following Donald Trump's victory, exemplifies an "informational moral panic." Using qualitative textual analysis, he draws out four major themes. The first focused on producers of misinformation, in which journalists drew explicit contrasts between their own motivations (to inform the public) and those of misinformation producers (to make money). The second theme showcases the role of social media platforms in facilitating the spread of "fake news" and enabling a "free-for-all" information environment that makes it impossible for consumers to tell fact from fiction. The third theme also critiques the internet, this time for the extent to which its click-driven profit model allows platforms to financially benefit from the spread of misinformation. Finally, the fourth theme excoriates gullible social media users for believing and sharing unverified information. Social media plays an outsize role in three out of four of these themes, both as a conduit for misinformation and as an existential crisis for traditional media. As Carlson explains, "the threat accorded to ["fake news"] by journalists reflects a fear that digital media channels only pollute the media environment, with an irresistible psychological and emotional draw that runs counter to standard objective news."

Drawing on a sample of articles about "fake news" published in Denmark during 2019, Farkas (2023) reaches a similar conclusion. Journalists, he argues, frame misinformation as evidence of the critical importance of the news media: "In the face of rapid technological change and financial hardship, fake news affirms the need to preserve the authority of established journalism as a societal knowledge gatekeeper." A more recent analysis of US coverage of deepfakes again finds a similar theme: while focusing on the "worst-case" scenario of deepfakes (a massively misinformed public), journalists also reify their own status as a bulwark against these threats (Wahl-Jorgensen and Carlson 2021), even in the face of increasing evidence that deepfakes may not be uniquely persuasive (Barari, Lucas and Munger 2021). Finally, Egelhofer et al. (2020) track journalists' use of the term "fake news" over a three-year period in eight major Austrian newspapers, including references to "fake news" as a type of misinformation (57% of articles), as a label to attack the news media (22% of articles), and as a synonym for anything false (43% of articles). The plurality of articles that mentioned who was responsible for counteracting "fake news" named social media (26%).

Despite employing quite different methodologies and different samples, these studies suggest a common theme in the media's treatment of the misinformation phenomenon. First, even though "fake news" circulates through a range of channels, including email chains, interpersonal conversation, text chats (e.g. WhatsApp) and mainstream media (including cable news), the media consistently portray social media as the primary bogeyman in their discussions of "fake news." And second, the mainstream media often explicitly contrasts the information free-for-all of social media with their own more systematic approach to fact-checking and verification.

2.1 Content Analysis Design and Procedure

This section presents the results of a content analysis designed to identify both themes in media coverage of misinformation and changes in the volume of coverage over time. The content analysis was conducted in two waves. The first wave, collected in 2019, examined media coverage from 2015 to 2018. These results informed the design of the experimental treatments. In 2023, the content analysis was updated to include data from 2019 to 2022, providing a comprehensive overview of media coverage that spans two presidencies and the COVID-19 pandemic. This date range was selected because it encompasses the rise of the "misinformation" phenomenon. *The Washington Post* aptly illustrates this dramatic shift in focus. In the thirty-five years prior to 2015, the words "misinformation" or "fake news" appeared in only 21 total *Washington Post* headlines – about one article every eighteen months. In the eight years that followed, these terms appeared in 200 headlines: about one every two weeks.

To systematically analyze media coverage of the misinformation phenomenon, I use the NexisUni and ProQuest databases to generate a list of all news articles whose headlines used the terms "misinformation" or "fake news" published in *The New York Times*, *Washington Post*, the *USA Today*, and the Associated Press between January 1, 2015, and January 1, 2019 (Phase 1) and between January 2, 2019, and December 31, 2023 (Phase 2). The first three publications have the highest circulations in the United States, and the AP provides content for local news outlets across the country.

I distinguish between these two phases of data collection and coding because the first set of articles was coded by two research assistants in 2020, and the results directly informed the design of the experiments in the following chapters. The second set of articles was coded by a different set of research assistants in 2023, with the goal of bringing the content analysis up to date and integrating coverage of the COVID pandemic. More information about inter-coder reliability for both phases is available in Section 2.1.4.

Selecting news articles that use the phrase in the *headline* (rather than only in the body of the text) ensures that the articles are about the larger phenomenon of misinformation, and avoids articles in which misinformation is mentioned only in passing and/or as a synonym for any kind of false belief.[1] While this sampling strategy avoids false positives, it also ignores articles about misinformation that do not explicitly mention the issue in the headline. For example, while a 2018 *USA Today* article headlined "Clock Ticking for Facebook to Halt Election Meddling" discusses Facebook's responsibility to stop the spread of "fake news" (Guynn 2018), this article is not included in the articles coded because it does not include either of the key phrases in its headline. In sum, while limiting the analysis to articles that are explicitly about misinformation and "fake news" limits the universe of articles to a more manageable size and makes it possible to observe patterns in how the media frame this emerging issue, this approach is limited in its ability to paint a complete picture of how these outlets discuss the topic.

Despite these limitations, it is also worth noting that headlines play an increasingly important role in news consumption. The "endless feed" of scrollable posts and headlines enabled by platforms like Facebook and X (formerly known as Twitter) makes it possible for users to consume news in "headline-only" format far more easily than before the advent of these platforms (Searles and Feezell 2023). Indeed, in 2018, 69% of Americans reported that they "scanned the headlines of a lot of stories" at least once a day (NORC 2018).

I focus on the specific terms "fake news" and "misinformation" because they are heavily used in public discourse about the topic. For example, Pew and Gallup's survey questions on the issue employ the term "misinformation." A robustness check shows that "misinformation" and "fake news" are indeed substantially more common than other terms: even when the headline search is expanded to include "post-truth," "alternative facts," and "false news," headlines employing "fake news" and misinformation make up 92% of the total articles in the sample. Of course, "misinformation" is itself a contested concept, and an active scholarly conversation has arisen around defining the term, along with similar concepts like conspiracy theories, rumors, disinformation, and "fake news" (Jerit and Zhao 2020; Vraga and Bode 2020). A key point of contention in this debate is the role of *intentionality*; in particular to what extent these different terms imply and/or require a deliberate attempt to deceive (Tandoc, Lim and Ling 2018). Because this study attempts to understand the patterns and effects of media coverage of the topic, I do not propose a rigid definition of "misinformation" or "fake news" but rather seek to analyze the range of (often contradictory) ways this fluid concept is discussed in mainstream

---

[1] For example, a 2018 AP article described how a Spirit Airlines flight attendant, "misinformed" about airline policy, told a passenger to flush her emotional support hamster down the toilet (The Associated Press 2018).

media.However, as the content analysis demonstrates, this idea of *responsibility* emerges in journalistic discourse as well, albeit slightly differently than in academic work.

The next section discusses the three types of content the news coverage was coded for: attribution of responsibility, the use of "fake news" as a rhetorical strategy, and (starting in 2020) references to COVID-related misinformation.

2.1.1 Attributing Responsibility for Misinformation to Social Media

The media play a critical role in shaping public beliefs about who is responsible for social problems (Iyengar 1994). Attributions of responsibility matter for democratic functioning, shaping both voting behavior (Marsh and Tilley 2010) and policy preferences (McGlynn and McGlone 2019). In the case of misinformation, social media is an easy scapegoat.

The tendency to hold social media primarily responsible for the misinformation epidemic is omnipresent in public discourse, including elite rhetoric. In the fall of 2018, Congress held a series of hearings specifically aimed at addressing the issue of fake news on social media, and called the CEOs of Facebook and Twitter to testify. A dislike of misinformation – and a tendency to blame social media for it – is one of few issues that both Democrats and Republicans can agree on. In 2022, Democrat Amy Klobuchar and Republican Cynthia Lummis introduced bipartisan legislation aimed at reducing misinformation-related harms of social media: "For too long, tech companies have said 'Trust us, we've got this.' But social media platforms have repeatedly put profits over people, with algorithms pushing dangerous content that hooks users and spreads misinformation" (Kelly 2022).

The public is also suspicious of social media's role in the misinformation epidemic, with 89% of Americans saying that social media is mostly or partly responsible for the spread of "fake news" (Murray 2018). In a 2022 study, Lima, Han and Cha (2022) use both open-ended and closed-ended questions to investigate who the public holds responsible for creating, disseminating, and failing to prevent misinformation. The majority (63%) of respondents held social media primarily responsible for failing to prevent the spread of misinformation, and 39% held them primarily responsible for disseminating it. Fewer (21.2%) believed that they were responsible for creating misinformation. These patterns did not differ between liberals and conservatives.

To investigate the extent to which media coverage blames social media for the misinformation epidemic, the content of each article was coded for whether it mentioned misinformation and/or "fake news" as a problem either caused by or endemic to social media. This category includes both mentions of specific platforms (e.g. Twitter or Facebook) as well as more general mentions of social media. However, it does not include mentions of "the internet" more broadly.

2.1.2 "Fake News" as Rhetorical Strategy

Soon after winning the 2016 presidential election, Donald Trump first used the term "fake news" to criticize news coverage that he personally disagreed with (Kurtzleben 2017; Ross and Rivers 2018; Funke 2018*b*). "Fake news" soon became a regular part of Trump's rhetoric (Lischka 2019; Meeks 2020): in the first six months of 2017, the Trump Twitter Archive shows that his tweets employed the term "fake news" about once every three days. The list of targets Trump has labeled as "fake news" includes specific outlets like CNN, *The Washington Post*, and *The New York Times*, as well as broader claims like negative job reports, allegations about collusion with Russia, and leaks from the White House (Britzky 2017). Trump's use of the term was in turn adopted by others, including both political elites and members of the public.

This use of "fake news" differs substantially from how many researchers use the term (for example, Allcott and Gentzkow (2017) define "fake news" as "news articles that are intentionally and verifiably false, and could mislead readers"). Egelhofer and Lecheler (2019) explicitly distinguish between the academic use of the term, which they call "the fake news *genre* (i.e. the deliberate creation of pseudojournalistic disinformation)" and the use of the term as a critique, which they refer to as "the fake news *label* (i.e. the instrumentalization of the term to delegitimize news media)." Understanding the extent to which this rhetoric is amplified via news coverage is especially important given that most Americans do not use Twitter, and most of those who do use the platform do not follow Donald Trump (Bacon Jr and Mehta 2018). Therefore, mainstream media coverage of the "fake news label" may be a primary channel through which many Americans are exposed to "fake news" as a rhetorical delegitimization strategy (Zhang et al. 2018; Farhall et al. 2019; Wells et al. 2020).

The content of each article was coded for whether it included any use of "fake news" as a delegitimization strategy. This included direct reporting on Trump's use of the term, its use by others (including Trump's supporters or other political actors), as well as attempts to analyze and/or refute the "fake news" label (Lischka 2019). For example, a 2017 *New York Times* article discussed how Russia's foreign ministry had begun characterizing news articles it disagreed with as "fake news" (MacFarquhar 2017).

2.1.3 COVID-related Misinformation

The COVID-19 pandemic began in January of 2020, immediately spurring concerns about – and research into – the spread of misinformation, including untested treatments, conspiracy theories, and false claims about the eventual COVID vaccine (Ball and Maxmen 2020; Porter, Velez and Wood 2023). Understanding the extent to which COVID misinformation was covered in mainstream news is important for several reasons. First, it provides an illuminating case study of how the media covers an emerging issue through the lens of misinformation. Second, it speaks to concerns that in its enthusiasm to debunk false claims, mainstream media might inadvertently amplify fringe false claims that originated on social media and initially had quite small audiences (Wardle 2018).

The content of each article published after January 2020 was coded for whether it included any mention of misinformation related to COVID-19. This included general mentions of COVID-related misinformation, as well as specific examples (e.g. false claims about the vaccine).

2.1.4 Coding Procedure and Validity

The initial NexisUni/ProQuest search generated 1,155 articles across the four outlets during the eight-year time period. All duplicate articles (e.g. versions published both online and in print that thus appeared multiple times in the database) were removed, along with letters to the editor, leaving a final sample of 859 articles. Each of the 859 articles was read and coded by two separate coders, both research assistants. Both used the same codebook (available in the Appendix), with the COVID section added for the second phase. The codebook provided an explicit definition, along with examples, of each category. Coders first coded a batch of 20 articles, then met to discuss any discrepancies before coding the remainder independently. Because the articles were collected four years apart (Phase 1 in 2019 and Phase 2 in 2023), different teams of coders read each of the two sets.

Table 1 shows the intercoder reliability for each of the three major themes: social media as responsible, the use of "fake news" as a rhetorical delegitimization strategy, and COVID-related misinformation.

Overall, reliability was quite high across all three categories for both the 347 articles published in 2015 through 2018 and for the 512 articles published in 2019 through 2023. While reliability was lowest (0.71) for use of "fake news" rhetoric in the second phase, all values were above the generally acceptable threshold of 0.60 (Landis and Koch 1977).

Table 1 Intercoder reliability.

	Social media		"Fake news" rhetoric		COVID misinfo	
	Agreement	Kappa	Agreement	Kappa	Agreement	Kappa
Phase 1 (2015–2018)	92%	0.80	96%	0.88	N/A	N/A
Phase 2 (2019–2022)	92%	0.79	98%	0.71	92%	0.83

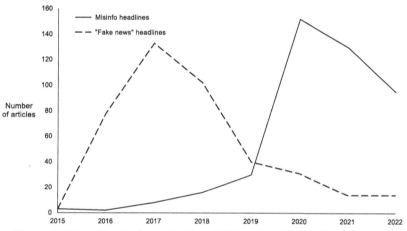

Figure 1 Use of "misinformation" and "fake news" in headlines by year.

2.2 Content Analysis Results

2.2.1 Changes in Coverage over Time

Together, the four news outlets published a total of 859 articles with "fake news" and/or "misinformation" in their headlines between 2015 and 2022. Over the time period as a whole, the two terms were used at similar rates, with 48% of the headlines using "fake news," 50% using "misinformation," and 2% using both. However, as Figure 1 demonstrates, these averages mask a great deal of over-time variation – specifically, a steep post-2017 decline in the use of "fake news" and a commensurate increase in "misinformation." In the first phase of the content analysis (2016–2018), 91% of headlines used the term "fake news." In the second phase of the content analysis (2019–2022), this pattern was reversed: 80% of headlines referenced "misinformation." This pattern was consistent across all four news outlets.

There are several potential reasons for this shift in terminology. As Donald Trump began to use the term more frequently, some journalists expressed increasing reluctance to employ it. In 2017, the nonprofit media institute Poynter published an article (directed at media practitioners) titled "Should We Stop Saying 'Fake News'?" The article laid out several arguments for why journalists should stop using the term, including concerns that the term had become "too weaponized to be useful" and its "definitional ambiguity" (Funke 2017). Similarly, in 2018, *Newsweek* published an opinion piece taking an even firmer stance, declaring "the term undermines the intellectual values of democracy— and there is a real possibility that it means nothing. We would be better off if we stopped using it" (Habgood-Coote 2018). While not everyone in the media community agreed with this recommendation (Meyer 2018), the results of the content analysis suggest that many journalists may have taken these warnings seriously.

A second reason that "misinformation" may have replaced "fake news" as the term of choice is increased concern over types of misinformation that are not masquerading as news articles. While much of the public discourse following the 2016 election focused on misinformation that was disguised as traditional news (Allcott and Gentzkow 2017), in the years that followed misinformation increasingly took other forms. For example, a 2020 AP article about COVID misinformation described false claims that do not fit neatly into the "fake news" paradigm: "Twitter users are also pushing YouTube video links that describe the coronavirus as a hoax … Facebook groups are peppered with posts that predict the government will force people to get coronavirus vaccinations and videos that say health officials are intentionally inflating coronavirus death numbers" (Seitz 2020).

2.2.2 Changes in Volume and Themes

Figure 2 shows the main results of the content analysis, illustrating both the trends in volume and theme of media coverage of misinformation. The patterns suggest that the surge in media attention to the misinformation phenomenon was in large part a reaction to the 2016 election. Of the 79 articles on the topic published in 2016, all but three came out *after* Trump's victory, and 2017 saw a total of 143 headlines about misinformation and/or "fake news." Coverage wanes slightly, with just 73 articles in 2019, and then increases dramatically in 2020 in the face of both COVID and a presidential election.

Of course, the sampling strategy under-represents the total volume of coverage, because it by design focuses on articles explicitly *about* the topic of misinformation. Many more articles mention the issue in passing. For example,

Table 2 Headline mentions of issues, 2015–2023.

Headline mention	Number of articles
Immigration	3648
Unemployment	2617
Misinformation or fake news	**1155**
Poverty	758
Inequality	528
National/federal debt/deficit	86

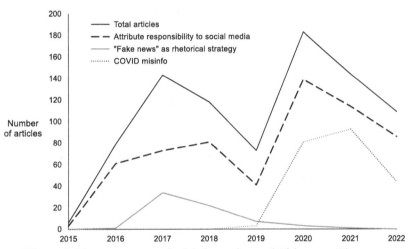

Figure 2 News coverage of misinformation and "fake news" by year.

in 2021, *The New York Times* ran 65 articles with "misinformation" in the headline, but 1,611 articles that included the word elsewhere in the article.

Because these raw numbers can be difficult to interpret, it is helpful to benchmark this volume of coverage to other relevant topics in the news. Table 2 shows the total number of headlines across the four outlets with each keyword in the title.[2] Misinformation and/or "fake news" are mentioned in headlines more frequently than the national/federal debt/deficit, poverty, or inequality, and less than half as often as immigration or unemployment. While these are noisy estimates, they provide a sense of the scope of coverage as compared to other issues of interest to the public.

---

[2] Issues were chosen based on common responses to the Gallup "most important problem" survey question. To facilitate comparability across categories, each of these categories is a simple raw count, without removing duplicates, letters to the editor, or irrelevant uses of the term.

Across the eight years, more than two-thirds (69%) of articles assigned blame to social media for the spread of misinformation and "fake news." Coverage in the Associated Press was least likely to blame social media (58%), while that in *The New York Times* was most likely to do so (75%). In many of the articles that blamed social media, the platforms were implicated in the headline itself. For example, a 2018 Associated Press headline read "Social Media and Misinformation: It's a Game of Whack-a-Mole," while a 2020 *New York Times* headline warned, "Misinformation Surge on Coronavirus Stumps Facebook and Twitter." In total, about one out of every seven articles during this time period implicated social media *in the headline itself,* making it possible even for casual news consumers to receive a clear signal about who was to blame for the problem.

While excoriations of social media were common, references to or uses of the term "fake news" as rhetorical delegitimization were far less frequent. Among the 778 articles published after Trump began using the phrase "fake news" in December 2017, just 9% (68) referenced him (or others) using the term in this way. A 2017 *USA Today* article headlined "Trump is Confident, Combative with Media; President-elect Blisters 'Fake News' Coverage" repeats a number of Trump's tweets using the phrase. Coverage in the Associated Press was least likely to reference the "fake news" delegitimization strategy (6%), while that in *The Washington Post* was most likely to do so (15%).

After the COVID pandemic began in early 2020, it quickly became a mainstay of misinformation coverage. In 2020 through 2022, fully 50% of misinformation stories mentioned specific pieces of COVID-related misinformation, including false claims about vaccines, masking, and unproven treatments. Stories that mentioned COVID-related misinformation were substantially more likely to also assign responsibility to social media than those that did not. Among the 2020–2022 articles that discussed COVID misinformation, 82% blamed social media, compared to 72% of stories without COVID mentions.

The content analysis offers empirical evidence that coverage of misinformation and "fake news" has indeed increased over the past four years, and that the majority of news coverage characterizes the issue as a problem endemic to social media in particular. These results echo journalists' larger concerns about social media: 67% of surveyed journalists think that social media has a negative impact on journalism (Gottfried et al. 2022). In addition, "fake news" as a rhetorical strategy comprised a minority of coverage, especially after 2018. Both these patterns are important for theorizing about how media attention to misinformation might shape public opinion, as well as for designing an experiment that accurately reflects media coverage of misinformation.

Finally, it is important to note that although many of these news stories imply that misinformation is more consequential than ever before, research supporting this assumption is limited. Jamieson (2020) shows how Russian trolls and hackers strategically spread misinformation in an attempt to influence the 2016 election, but little empirical evidence suggests that these attempts had large effects on voters' attitudes and/or behavior. Survey data paired with web traffic from the 2016 election suggests that most Americans did not see any "fake news" websites, and those who did visited only a few (Guess, Nyhan and Reifler 2020). Similarly, an analysis of Twitter data suggests that the vast majority of "fake news" exposures was concentrated among 1% of users (Grinberg et al. 2019). When people do visit "fake news" sites, they are overwhelmingly like-minded ones that likely reinforce rather than change attitudes (Guess, Nyhan and Reifler 2020), and experimental participants randomly assigned to read "fake news" stories show little change in opinion (Guess et al. 2020). Thus, while evidence suggests that both the absolute reach and persuasive power of "fake news" on social media is (as of yet) relatively small (Allcott and Gentzkow 2017; Guess, Nyhan and Reifler 2018; Nyhan 2020), journalism *about* fake news – and in particular, about the role of social media in spreading misinformation – has seen substantial growth.

3 Potential Effects of News Coverage of Misinformation

While a large literature has examined the effects of direct exposure to misinformation and "fake news" (Nyhan 2010; Pasek, Sood and Krosnick 2015; Thorson 2016; Berinsky 2017; Wood and Porter 2019), fewer studies have examined how the ways the mass media has covered the issue might also shape public opinion (though see Tsfati et al. (2020)). This section outlines specific hypotheses about how media coverage of misinformation might affect beliefs and attitudes.

3.1 Effects on Estimates of the Prevalence of Misinformation

First, exposure to heavy coverage of the "fake news" phenomenon likely affects peoples' estimates of how much misinformation is present in the media environment. Just as watching news stories about crime increases viewers' estimates of both the overall crime rate and their own risk of becoming a victim of violent crime (Lowry, Nio and Leitner 2003; Romer, Jamieson and Aday 2003), seeing news about misinformation may increase peoples' estimates of how frequently they or others are exposed to misinformation. This effect is driven in part by the "availability heuristic": people's estimates of the size of a particular category (e.g. crimes in their area or misinformation in the media) is affected by how easily they can bring examples to mind (Riddle 2010; Kahneman 2011). Thus, H1 predicts that exposure to news coverage of misinformation increases estimates of exposure to misinformation.

Of course, most Americans already believe misinformation is quite common: in 2018, they estimated that about 39% of the news on "television, newspapers, and on the radio" was misinformation, along with 65% of news on social media (Gallup 2018). Given these differences between media types, RQ1 asks whether exposure to news about misinformation shapes estimates of misinformation differently for television, print news, and social media. For example, does reading about the "fake news" phenomenon increase estimates of misinformation on social media more than it does estimates of misinformation on television?

3.2 Effects on Trust in Media

The decline in media trust over the past few decades, especially among Republicans, has been an increasing matter of concern for pundits and academics alike (Ladd and Podkul 2018; Stephens 2023). Evidence suggests that direct exposure to misinformation leads to less trust in media: among participants who installed a browser extension tracking their web visits over a three-month period, those who saw more "fake news" also showed a larger decrease in media trust (Ognyanova et al. 2020). Survey data also suggests that those who self-report having heard about more "fake news" stories become less trusting in media over time (Lee, Gil de Zúñiga and Munger 2023). In addition, participants randomly assigned to learn about a conspiracy theory became more skeptical of the information environment (Invernizzi and Mohamed 2023).

To what extent might we expect a similar effect for news coverage about misinformation? This section discusses two different channels through which news coverage of misinformation could accelerate this decline in media trust. First, it might serve to bring attention to (even if inadvertently) Donald Trump's rhetorical strategy of discrediting mainstream media by calling it "fake news." Second, highlighting the surfeit of misinformation might decrease citizens' trust in the information environment more broadly.

Concerns over the public's decline in media trust were amplified when, in 2016, Trump adopted the term "fake news" as a one-size-fits-all critique of any information he disagreed with. Indeed, in 2016, then-presidential candidate Donald Trump explicitly stated that he deliberately attempted to discredit journalists "so that when you write negative stories about me, no one will believe you" (CBSNews 2018). While the content analysis shows that Trump's explicit attacks comprised a minority of "fake news" and misinformation coverage, these attacks may still have an indirect effect on media trust by creating an implicit association between misinformation and mainstream journalism. Indeed, Van Duyn and Collier (2018) find that experimental participants randomly assigned to view tweets from elites using the term "fake news" had lower levels of media trust, although the effect was small and inconsistent across studies.

News coverage of misinformation may also decrease trust through a different mechanism: the belief that misinformation is omnipresent may increase overall skepticism, which may in turn impact evaluations even of trustworthy content. This effect is consistent with other interventions that attempt to raise awareness about misleading content. For example, viewing a warning that some stories may "use misleading tactics to try and convince the public they are true" reduces belief not only in false news stories but also in true ones (Clayton et al. 2019), learning that a video is a "deepfake" decreases trust in social media (Vaccari and Chadwick 2020), and reading a warning about misinformation decreases the perceived credibility of accurate headlines (van der Meer, Hameleers and Ohme 2023).

Given the consistent negative effect of both direct exposure to misinformation and exposure to fact-checks and warnings on media trust, H2 predicts that exposure to news coverage of misinformation will decrease media trust. However, this effect is by no means inevitable. The results of the content analysis in this Element, as well as several previous examinations of media coverage of "fake news" (Carlson 2020; Egelhofer et al. 2020; Farkas 2023), suggest that journalists actively (and perhaps strategically) blame social media for misinformation partly to reify their own positions as informational gatekeepers. If their effort is successful, then exposure to misinformation coverage may actually *increase* trust in mainstream media.

3.3 Effects on Political Trust

By bringing attention to the problem of misinformation, news coverage may also decrease political trust more generally (Lazer et al. 2018). Survey research suggests that about a third of Americans explicitly hold politicians primarily responsible for the creation of misinformation (Lima, Han and Cha 2022), and so reading stories about the misinformation phenomenon may intensify their political cynicism and/or distrust of the political system. Exposure to fact-checking has a similar effect in terms of decreasing trust Pingree, Hill and McLeod (2013, p. 209) found that exposure to fact-checking increased political cynicism because it "highlights inaccurate or misleading claims by elites."

More recently, during the 2018 midterm elections, people who perceived themselves as being exposed to misinformation showed increased levels of political cynicism (Jones-Jang, Kim and Kenski 2021).

Testing the *causal* impact of misinformation coverage on political trust is important because these observed associations could also plausibly be driven by direct exposure to misinformation that critiques existing institutions (Bennett and Livingston 2018). H3 thus predicts that exposure to news coverage of misinformation decreases political trust.

3.4 Pretest: Identifying Headlines and Investigating Partisan Differences

In December 2018 (prior to Study 1), a pretest was conducted to address the possibility that Republicans and Democrats react differently to headlines about misinformation and/or those that use the term "fake news." Two factors make investigating these questions important. First, the term "fake news" may not be interchangeable with "misinformation" because it has been used strategically by President Trump as a critique of the mainstream news industry (Funke 2018*b*; Ott 2017). Second, at least in the 2016 election, misinformation itself was not distributed evenly along partisan lines: there was more fabricated content favoring conservative points of view (Guess, Nyhan and Reifler 2018). If media coverage of misinformation has been similarly asymmetrical, Republicans might react differently than Democrats to news about the topic. The pretest was thus designed to investigate, using both closed and open-ended responses, potential partisan differences in perceptions of (1) articles about misinformation and (2) the term "fake news" versus "misinformation." In addition, the design makes it possible to identify specific news headlines that are evaluated similarly by both Democrats and Republicans, and could be used as treatments in the experiment.

The pretest included 414 participants (52% Democratic and 48% Republican, identified via branching partisanship questions) recruited via Survey Sampling International (SSI). All participants indicated whether each of a set of twenty headlines (all taken from real news articles) favored Democrats, favored Republicans, or favored neither. The headlines, presented in random order, included eight about made-up news (e.g., "Facebook Will Now Fact-Check Photos, Videos as It Fights Misinformation") and twelve about elections more generally (e.g. "Campaigns Are Texting Voters Out of the Blue"). For half the respondents, the headlines about made-up news used the term "misinformation." The other half saw the same headlines but with the phrase "fake news" substituted. At the end of the survey, respondents answered a thought-listing question about one of the misinformation/fake news headlines they had seen earlier. Specifically, they were shown the headline again and asked, "What comes to mind when you see this headline?"

3.4.1 Pretest Results: No Evidence of Partisan Differences

Respondents do not perceive stories about misinformation as having more partisan bias than stories about politics. Averaging across the twelve non-misinformation headlines, 55% (S.D. = 8.4) of respondents answered that the story "favors neither party," compared to 47% for the misinformation headlines (S.D. = 5.0), a statistically indistinguishable difference. In addition, Republicans were no more likely than Democrats to perceive misinformation stories as biased.[3] On average, Republicans perceived 15% of the politics headlines and 14% of the headlines about made-up news as biased towards Democrats. Table 3 shows the full list of headlines used in the pretest, along with the percent of respondents who reported that each headline favored Republicans, favored Democrats, or favored neither party.

The term used to describe false information does not affect perceptions of partisan bias, either among respondents as a whole or partisans in particular. Perceived partisan bias is identical regardless of whether the headline uses the term "fake news" or "misinformation," both for the sample as a whole and for Republicans.

As an additional measure of perceived partisan bias, the open-ended responses were coded for any references to partisanship or partisan figures.[4] Overall, just 16% of the open-ended responses specifically mentioned partisanship or partisan bias: a relatively low number given that the idea of partisan bias was explicitly primed in the headline evaluation task that respondents completed immediately before answering the open-ended question. Table 4 shows that the only factor significantly associated with making a partisan reference is political interest. This pattern is consistent with Krupnikov and Ryan's (2022) argument that level of political engagement is often a more meaningful predictor of behavior than partisan identification. Finally, respondents assigned to the "fake news" condition were not more likely to make a partisan reference, nor were Republicans. There was also not a significant interaction between the two.

---

[3] I describe the data here in terms of overall distribution for ease of interpretation and discussion. However, the Appendix also includes details of a regression analysis in which the dependent variable is the difference between the average perceived bias of the misinformation articles versus control articles. The results are the same: there is neither a main effect of party ID nor use of the term "fake news," nor is there a significant interaction between the two.

[4] For example, "Censorship of conservative views," "Who else...the Donald," and "the president trying to get attention."

Table 3 Perceptions that headlines favor a party.

Control headlines	Democrats	Neither	Republicans
Traditional Election Maps Don't Tell the Full Story	25.8	50.7	23.5
Four Steps to Protect Our Elections	25.6	53.3	21.0
Election Uncertainty Spurs Investors to Hedge	24.9	52.8	22.3
Young Voters Could Sway Election, If They Turn Up	53.7	39.4	6.9
Campaigns Are Texting Voters Out of the Blue	28.8	52.4	18.9
Posting Political Signs in the Window Is Your Right — Isn't It?	20.9	61.7	17.3
Advertising War Already Started during Tough Election Season	28.0	53.7	18.3
Viral Videos Are Replacing Pricey Political Ads	25.4	61.9	12.7
after a Tough 2016, Many Pollsters Haven't Changed Anything	26.7	51.4	21.9
New Voting Machines Will Provide "Paper Trail"	19.9	59.2	20.9
Wandering Voters Key to Presidential Race	26.9	53.0	20.1
Wisconsin Couple Has Dueling Political Yard Signs	13.2	74.5	12.3
Average	**26.7**	**55.3**	**18.0**
Misinfo/Fake News headlines	**Democrats**	**Neither**	**Republicans**
Experts Tell Senate Panel [Misinformation/Fake News] Campaigns Are Growing More Sophisticated	25.8	48.3	25.8

Table 3 (*Cont.*)

Misinfo/Fake News headlines	Democrats	Neither	Republicans
Political Ignorance and the Future of Political [Misinformation/Fake News] Online	27.2	47.1	25.7
How Twitter Is Being Gamed to Feed [Misinformation/Fake News]	31.7	44.7	23.6
Fighting [Misinformation/Fake News] on Social Media Has Proven Lucrative for Tech Groups	25.7	52.9	21.5
Facebook Will Now Fact-Check Photos, Videos as It Fights [Misinformation/Fake News]	27.3	54.1	18.5
[Misinformation/Fake News] on Social Media Platforms Is a New Kind of Cybersecurity Attack, Expert Says	28.4	53.5	18.1
How Can Students Learn to Distinguish [Misinformation/Fake News] from Real News?	23.3	59.5	17.2
Google Announces Plan to Combat Spread of [Misinformation/Fake News]	29.8	55.8	14.4
Average	**27.4**	**52.0**	**20.6**

Taken together, the results of the pretest indicate that people do not perceive stories about misinformation as more biased than stories about politics in general. While Republicans perceive *all* stories as more biased towards Democrats than vice versa (consistent with Republicans' overall distrust of media), this effect is not magnified when the story is about misinformation. The term used

Table 4 Factors associated with invoking partisanship
in the open-ended response.

	Partisan reference	
Female	0.62	(0.19)
Age	1.24	(0.15)
Education	0.94	(0.083)
Political interest	1.79***	(0.31)
Republican	1.90	(0.77)
Fake news condition	1.10	(0.42)
Republican × Fake news	1.17	(0.67)
Observations	405	
Pseudo R^2	.081	

Exponentiated coefficients; Standard errors in parentheses
$^* p < 0.05$, $^{**} p < 0.01$, $^{***} p < 0.001$

to describe false information (misinformation vs. "fake news") also does not affect perceptions of partisan bias, either among respondents as a whole or partisans in particular. The pretest directly informed the design of Study 1 (outlined in the next section) in two major ways. First, the results provide empirical evidence that using both "fake news" and "misinformation" in the headlines is unlikely to introduce a problematic interaction with partisanship. Second, the specific headlines tested (Table 5) were used in Study 1's treatment.

4 Study 1: How Misinformation Coverage Shapes Perceptions and Trust

Study 1 measures the effects of exposure to news coverage of misinformation by randomly assigning participants to read either headlines about misinformation and "fake news," headlines about politics and elections more generally, or a control condition (no headlines). Using headlines rather than asking people to read full articles is designed to increase external validity by replicating the context in which people are exposed to news coverage of misinformation: often not in a context-rich, detailed article, but in succinct headlines. News consumers increasingly see news in headline format (for example, in their Facebook news feeds) rather than as longer pieces, and exposure to news only in headline format may be especially common for people who are the least interested in politics (Gabielkov et al. 2016; Bode, Vraga and Troller-Renfree 2017). Thus, while showing respondents a series of headlines may be a weaker treatment

Table 5 Headlines used in Study 1.

Election headlines
Election Uncertainty Spurs Investors to Hedge
Campaigns Are Texting Voters Out of the Blue
Posting Political Signs in the Window Is Your Right - Isn't It?
Advertising War Already Started during Tough Election Season
After A Tough 2016, Many Pollsters Haven't Changed Anything
Wandering Voters Key to Presidential Race
Misinformation headlines
Fighting Misinformation on Social Media Has Proven Lucrative for Tech Groups
Facebook Will Now Fact-Check Photos, Videos as It Fights Misinformation
Fake News on Social Media Platforms is a New Kind of Cybersecurity Attack
How Can Students Learn to Distinguish Misinformation from Real News?
Google Announces Plan to Combat Spread of Fake News
(One election-related headline inserted at random from the "Election Headlines" list)

than asking them to read a full news story about misinformation, it also more accurately replicates the reality of news exposure on the internet and reduces the likelihood that any observed effects are due to an artificial forced-exposure experimental format (Arceneaux and Johnson 2013).

4.1 Study 1 Design

An online survey (N=3,507) was conducted in the spring of 2019 via the survey vendor Lucid. Lucid uses quota sampling to match US census demographics, and participants recruited via Lucid perform similarly to representative samples on several experimental benchmark surveys (Coppock and McClellan 2019). The sample was evenly split between men and women. Twenty-three percent were age thirty or under, 27% between 31 and 45, 27% between 46 and 60, and 24% over the age of 60. 36% identified as Democrats, 28% as Republicans, and 34% as Independents. A quarter of the sample had a bachelor's degree, and 23% have a high school diploma or less. The median survey completion time was 7.2 minutes, and no respondents who completed the survey were excluded from the analysis.

Participants were first asked their age and gender. They then completed two batteries to be used as potential covariates, and thus asked prior to treatment (Montgomery, Nyhan and Torres 2018). The first consisted of four agree-disagree questions measuring their general predisposition to conspiratorial thinking (α = .81, 1-5 scale, M = 3.2, SD = .97) (Uscinski, Klofstad and Atkinson 2016). The second question measured media consumption, asking participants how often (never, sometimes, often) they got news from the following sources: Facebook, Twitter, Fox News, local TV news, national TV news, MSNBC, online news websites, and print newspapers. Finally, to assess political interest, they were asked, "how closely do you follow what's going on in government and public affairs?" (1–4 scale, M=3.0).

Participants were then randomly assigned to one of three conditions: a "misinformation headlines" condition, an "election headlines" condition, and a pure control group. The first two groups were told, "Different people prefer different types of news stories. We're interested in learning more about the types of news you prefer." They were then asked to rate their interest in six different headlines. In the "misinformation headlines" condition, five out of the six headlines explicitly referenced the issue of misinformation, and the sixth was about elections more generally. In the "election headlines" condition, the six headlines were all about US elections and did not reference misinformation. The inclusion of both an "election headlines" condition and a pure control condition makes it possible to distinguish the effects of misinformation coverage from the effects of political coverage more generally. None of the headlines were attributed to a specific outlet.

Respondents in the pure control group did not see any headlines. Rather, they proceeded directly to the dependent variables. The inclusion of this group helps to establish a neutral baseline against which to compare effects of the misinformation treatment. In many survey experiments examining media effects in politics, the control group sees nonpolitical content For example, in Levendusky and Malhotra's (2016) study of how news coverage of polarization shapes attitudes, respondents in the control condition read an article about a popular television show. However, showing respondents nonpolitical headlines might also affect media trust, and so the inclusion of a pure control group helps to avoid this issue.

Table 5 shows the full list of headlines used in Study 1, all of which are based on real news articles. Both the content analysis and the pretest informed the selection of headlines. The content analysis found that about two-thirds of news coverage held social media partially or fully responsible for the spread of "fake news," and that many articles implicated social media in the headline itself. Similarly, three out of the five headlines used in the experimental treatment

Advertising War Already Started During Tough Election Season

Not at all
interesting

0	1	2	3	4	5	6	7	8	9	10

Very
interesting

Which of the following statements best describes what this story is about?

O Candidates have already started running ads for the next election
O Candidates have started taking their spouses with them on the campaign trail

Figure 3 Example of headline and questions.

mention social media. All of the headlines used in Study 1 were also part of the pretest, and each was perceived as equally unbiased by both Democrats and Republicans. Participants saw each headline on a separate page, and below each one was a question asking about their interest in the story and a brief factual question about the headline, which served to ensure that they were reading the headlines. An example, with the accompanying questions, is shown in Figure 3.

Immediately after reading the headlines, participants completed a brief thought-listing task in which they were asked, "what thoughts came to mind when reading those headlines?" The question was designed to encourage more deliberation as well as to generate insights into the types of thoughts that people have about the topic of misinformation (Brewer and Gross 2005). Then, they completed the questions tapping the dependent variables of interest.

Perceptions of the prevalence of misinformation. All respondents indicated how often (every day, a few times a week, a few times a month, a few times a year, rarely or never) they themselves encountered misinformation (M = 4.0, SD = 1.2). In addition, given the extent to which the third-person effect shapes concerns over misinformation (Altay and Acerbi 2023), I also measure how often they think the average person encountered misinformation (M = 4.2, SD = 1.0). They also estimated the percentage of news that is misinformation (from 0 to 100) on social media (M = 62.4, SD = 24.6), TV (M = 50.3, SD = 27.2), and in newspapers (M = 40.8, SD = 25.7).

Trust in media. Trust in media was assessed with a battery of three different questions (α = .76, 1-4 scale, M = 2.6, SD = .70): how much of the time they could trust the media to report the news fairly, and how much (if at all) they trusted the information they got from national news and from local news.

Political trust. Political trust was measured with three agree-disagree state-ments: "Most politicians are trustworthy," "Politicians in the U.S. do not deserve much respect," and "Politicians generally have good intentions," as well as a question asking, "In general, how often can you trust the government in Washington to do what is right?" ($\alpha = .67$, 0–1 scale, M = .42, SD = .19)

Finally, participants answered a series of demographic questions including gender, income, education, and party identification, followed by an additional manipulation check.

4.2 Study 1 Results

4.2.1 Manipulation Checks

The experiment included two manipulation checks. Immediately after reading each headline, participants were asked to answer a question about the topic of the story. People in both the election and misinformation headline conditions answered an average of five out of the six questions correctly, suggesting that most participants paid relatively close attention to the experimental treatments, and that their attention did not differ by condition. The second manipulation check came at the end of the experiment. All participants who had been shown headlines (i.e. those not in the pure control group) were asked, "Were some of the headlines you saw earlier specifically about the issue of misinformation?" In the "elections headline" group, 53% answered affirmatively, compared to 90% in the treatment group.[5]

4.2.2 Descriptives: Who Perceives the Most Misinformation?

This section offers descriptive context about the types of people who self-report seeing more misinformation. Table 6 shows factors associated with higher levels of self-reported exposure to misinformation.[6]

Overall, people who are older, more politically interested, more educated, and higher in conspiratorial thinking all report seeing misinformation more frequently. These patterns could represent one of two phenomena: first, these groups may actually see more misinformation. Alternatively, however, these groups may have more previous exposure to narratives about misinforma-tion (e.g. the media coverage explored in the content analysis), which makes

---

[5] The many false positives in the election headlines group may be explained by the fact that immediately before the manipulation check, participants answered a battery of questions asking about the prevalence of misinformation.

[6] This pattern was similar when participants were asked about the "average person" rather than themself (see Table A3 in the Appendix), although (consistent with the third-person effect) the baseline estimates were slightly higher.

Table 6 Predictors of self-reported frequency of exposure to misinformation.

	Perceived exposure (self)	
Age	0.086**	(0.030)
Education	0.15***	(0.034)
Female	−0.11	(0.065)
Republican	0.22**	(0.079)
Independent	0.14	(0.076)
Political interest	0.33***	(0.040)
Conspiratorial thinking	0.16***	(0.028)
Constant	2.10***	(0.18)
Observations	1052	
Adjusted R^2	0.139	

Standard errors in parentheses

$^*p < 0.05$, $^{**}p < 0.01$, $^{***}p < 0.001$

them believe that misinformation is a larger problem. Finally, it is notable that Republicans are significantly more likely than Democrats to say that they see misinformation frequently.

4.2.3 Effects on Estimates of the Prevalence of Misinformation

H1 predicted that exposure to news coverage of misinformation would increase respondents' perceptions of misinformation's prevalence. Figure B.3 shows how the treatment affected respondents' estimates of how often the average person and they themselves were exposed to misinformation. The dependent variable is on a 1 (never) to 5 (every day) scale. As expected, reading headlines about misinformation significantly increased estimates of how much both they (B=.14, p<.01) and others (B=.17, p<.001) were exposed to misinformation.

RQ1 asked whether the treatment affected peoples' estimates of misinformation differently across media types. Participants were asked to estimate the percentage of the news on social media, television, and newspapers that is misinformation. Table 7 shows these estimates for the pure control condition (N=1,077). Consistent with previous research, people are most skeptical of news content on social media, estimating that about 60% of what they see on the platforms is misinformation (compared to 52% on television and 42% in newspapers). Republicans and Democrats are equally skeptical of social media content. However, they diverge more in their estimates of television and

Table 7 Estimates of percentage of news that is misinformation (pure control only).

	Total	Democrats	Republicans	Independents
Social media	**61.3%**	61.2%	61.6%	61.2%
Television	**51.9%**	47.4%	57.4%	52.2%
Newspapers	**42.2%**	38.8%	48.1%	41.0%

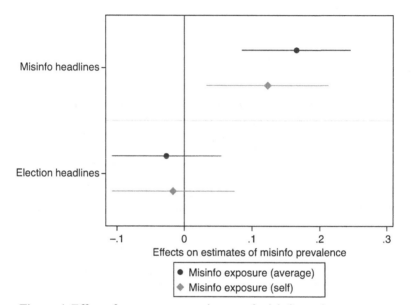

Figure 4 Effect of treatments on estimates of misinformation exposure.

news: for both these media, Republicans perceive more misinformation than Democrats (consistent with the partisan differences in Table 6.

But as Figure 5 shows, these estimates were affected in different ways by the treatment.[7] Compared to the respondents in the pure control condition, respondents who read the misinformation headlines offered *higher* estimates of misinformation on social media, and *lower* estimates of misinformation in newspapers and television. While the increased estimate for social media is perhaps unsurprising given that several of the headlines explicitly mentioned social media, the lower estimates for print and television (as compared to the control condition) suggests that exposure to media coverage of misinformation

---

[7] Covariates are omitted for visual clarity, but the full model is included in Appendix Table A6.

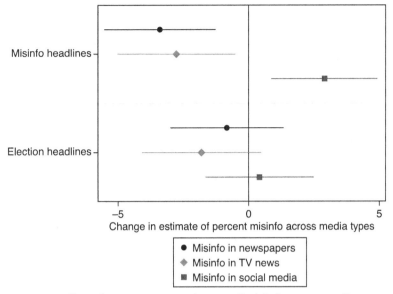

Figure 5 Effect of treatments on estimates of misinfo across media types.

may also actually *improve* perceptions of news quality in more traditional news sources.

4.2.4 Effects on Trust in Institutions

H2 predicted that exposure to news coverage of misinformation would decrease trust in media. However, Figure 6 shows that the opposite is true: people who saw the headlines about misinformation express *more* trust in media than those who saw the election headlines or those in the pure control group. The effect size is significant but relatively small, moving participants about .1 on a 4-point scale. To put this effect size in context, seeing the misinformation headlines increases media trust by about the same magnitude as moving one unit higher on the four-point conspiratorial thinking scale decreases media trust.

H3 predicted that news coverage of misinformation would decrease political trust. This hypothesis is not supported: as Figure 6 shows, viewing misinformation headlines has no effect on political trust.

Finally, as in the pretest, the open-ended responses were coded for references to partisan politics, including political figures. In total, just 3% of respondents made partisan references, and those in the "election" and "misinformation" conditions were equally likely to do so. These results again suggest that news coverage misinformation does not have a strong partisan charge.

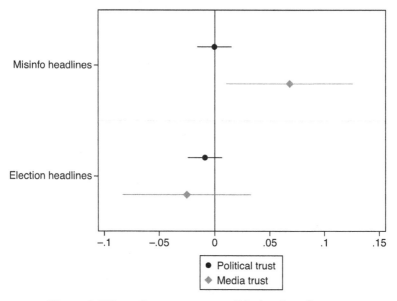

Figure 6 Effect of treatments on political and media trust.

4.2.5 Predictors of Interest in Misinformation Coverage

This study also provides some descriptive information about perceptions of headlines about misinformation. As part of the treatment, participants were asked to indicate how interesting they found each headline, on a scale of 1 to 10. Overall, respondents found the misinformation headlines substantially more interesting than the election news headlines, with an average interest level of 6.3 (SE=.07) versus 5.3 (SE=.07) for the election headlines. In addition, they wrote significantly longer responses to the open-ended thought-listing question following the misinformation articles than the election articles.

Table 8 shows some of the specific factors associated with interest in the control articles (about elections more generally) versus the treatment articles (about misinformation).

Some factors (Democratic Party identification, political interest) are associated with increased interest in both types of headlines. As we might expect, those higher in conspiratorial thinking find the misinformation headlines (but not the general election headlines) more compelling. Interestingly, older respondents are less interested in misinformation headlines than their younger counterparts. Taken together, these results offer some explanation for the media's intense focus on misinformation: audiences (especially those who are already politically interested) are highly engaged by stories about "fake news."

Table 8 Predictors of article interest.

	Interest in misinfo articles		Interest in control articles	
Age	−0.18**	(0.060)	0.050	(0.061)
Education	0.026	(0.069)	0.058	(0.069)
Female	−0.16	(0.13)	0.30*	(0.13)
Republican	0.022	(0.16)	−0.10	(0.17)
Democrat	0.34*	(0.15)	0.48**	(0.16)
Political interest	1.14***	(0.082)	0.82***	(0.086)
Conspiratorial thinking	0.14**	(0.054)	0.072	(0.057)
Constant	1.88***	(0.33)	3.08***	(0.35)
Observations	1016		1038	
Adjusted R^2	0.187		0.101	

Standard errors in parentheses

* $p < 0.05$, ** $p < 0.01$, *** $p < 0.001$

5 Study 2: Misinformation Coverage and Media Trust

Study 1 produced a surprising result: that exposure to news coverage of misinformation *increased* trust in media. However, Study 1 had several shortcomings. First, it employed a blunt measure of media trust that did not distinguish between different media types. Second, it was conducted on an opt-in online sample that may include heavier internet users than the general population (Guess and Munger 2023), which could in turn shape their assessments of and/or trust in online social media platforms. Third, Study 1 asked respondents their partisanship post-treatment, making it difficult to examine whether treatment effects were different for Democrats and Republicans. And finally, because several of Study 1's treatment headlines explicitly mentioned social media, they may have unintentionally primed respondents to hold social media responsible.

Study 2 was designed to reproduce the findings of Study 1 while also addressing its shortcomings. First, Study 2 uses a more fine-grained measure of media trust that distinguishes between news on print, television, and social media. Second, it employs a representative sample that includes participants who are not frequent internet users. Third, partisanship was collected in a previous wave of the survey, eliminating concerns about a measure of partisan identity either priming partisanship (if asked prior to treatment) or being affected by that treatment (if asked afterwards). Finally, Study 2 uses a non-headline operationalization of "news coverage of misinformation," instead embedding a cue about "recent news coverage of misinformation [on social media]" within a survey question.

I test two hypotheses: that increasing the salience of misinformation will decrease trust in news from social media (H1), and that it will increase trust in print news sources (H2). In addition, I examine whether these effects vary by partisanship (RQ1) and whether these effects vary depending on whether social media is explicitly mentioned in the cue (RQ2).

5.1 Study 2 Design

The study, a between-subjects question order experiment, was fielded via the Time-Sharing Experiments for the Social Sciences (TESS), using the AmeriSpeak panel, a nationally representative, probability-based panel. First, all 2,118 participants indicated how often they got news from a variety of sources, including print, television, and social media. They were also asked how closely they followed politics.

Participants in the treatment group were first asked the following question to cue them to think about news coverage of misinformation:

> Lately, there have been a lot of news stories about the spread of political misinformation [on social media]. How closely are you following news about this issue?

Half the respondents received the version of the question that read "the spread of political misinformation on social media," while the other half was asked just about "misinformation." They were then asked how trustworthy they found news from print (local newspapers and national newspapers), TV (local TV news and national TV news), and social media (Facebook and Twitter), and to estimate the percentage of misinformation in news on social media, newspapers, and television. The treatment consisted of the order in which the questions were asked: participants in the control group completed the trust battery and estimates first, and then saw the question about news coverage of misinformation.

5.2 Study 2 Results

Descriptives: Who Reports Following News about Misinformation?

Because the independent variable (salience of news coverage of misinformation) was embedded in a survey question, it can also yield useful information about what types of people self-report following news about misinformation.

Table 9 Predictors of self-reporting closely following news about misinformation.

	Following news about misinfo	
Age	−0.036**	(0.013)
Female	−0.041	(0.045)
Republican	−0.0083	(0.065)
Democrat	−0.00057	(0.063)
Political interest	0.69***	(0.030)
Education	0.049	(0.028)
Constant	0.52***	(0.12)
Observations	1044	
Adjusted R^2	0.371	

Standard errors in parentheses

$^*p < 0.05,$ $^{**}p < 0.01,$ $^{***}p < 0.001$

Table 9 shows factors associated with self-reporting following news about misinformation among those who were asked this question prior to answering questions about their trust in media and misinformation prevalence. The dependent variable is measured on a 1 (not at all) to 4 (very closely) scale (M=2.5, SE=.03).

The results closely parallel those in Study 1. Again, the strongest predictor of following news about misinformation is political interest, and there is a negative association with age. In addition, Republicans and Democrats were identical in their self-reported interest (M=2.7, SE=.19 for both), reinforcing the findings from Study 1 that there is not a partisan difference in appetite for misinformation news.

5.2.1 Effects on Estimates of Misinformation's Prevalence

As in Study 1, making news coverage of misinformation more salient significantly *decreased* respondents' estimates of the percentage of misinformation in print media, from 30.3% to 27.6%, $t(2056)=2.57, p=005$. However, as Figure 7 shows, it did not have a significant effect on their estimates of misinformation on social media or on television.

RQ2 asks whether explicitly mentioning "social media" in the misinformation coverage would change perceptions of prevalence. It did not: those who saw the "social media" version of the question then estimated that 56.9% of information on social media was misinformation, compared to 58.9% in the

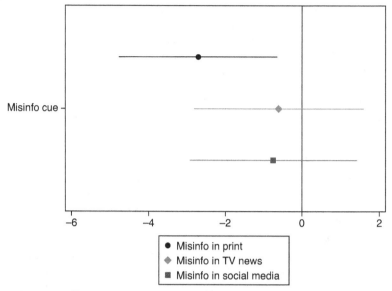

Figure 7 Effect of treatments on estimates of misinformation exposure.

non-social-media version. Similarly, the cue had no effect on estimates of prevalence in print media: participants who saw the social media cue estimated that 27.1% of print news was misinformation, compared to 28.1% in the no-cue condition. RQ2 also asked whether the inclusion of the "social media" cue affected media trust. Unsurprisingly, given that the cue did not affect estimates of prevalence, it did not have an impact on trust in print, social, or television news.

5.2.2 Effects on Media Trust

Hypotheses H1 and H2 predicted that as in Study 1, people who were reminded about news coverage of misinformation would be more trusting of print media and less trusting of social media. Figure 8 shows how exposure to the "news about misinformation" prompt affects trust across media types. The results are consistent with Study 1. Exposure to the misinformation coverage cue significantly decreases trust in social media. It also increases trust in print media (as compared to the control condition) by about the same amount as Republican identification (as compared to Independent) decreases it. In addition, there is not a significant interaction between Republican identification and the misinformation cue, suggesting that exposure to news about misinformation does not differentially affect Republicans' levels of trust in print media.

One of the strengths of Study 2 is that it offers a different operationalization of the independent variable (news coverage of misinformation) than in Study 1. While Study 1 showed respondents specific headlines, Study 2 merely primed

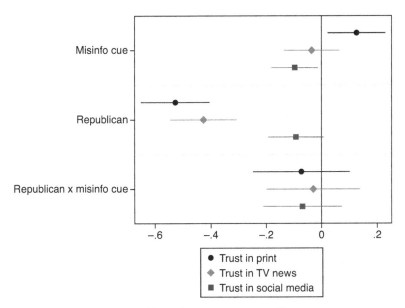

Figure 8 Effect of treatments on media trust.

the respondents to think about news coverage of misinformation. The fact that the effect of the misinformation coverage cue lowers trust in social media and raises trust in print media even when the word "social media" is not explicitly mentioned suggests that the public already has a strong association between misinformation and social media.

Despite the different treatments, the results of Study 2 parallel those in Study 1. Exposure increases estimates of misinformation on social media and decreases estimates of misinformation in mainstream news, with corresponding effects on trust. This similar pattern across both studies strongly suggests that the effects of misinformation coverage on trust are not driven solely by the fact that the Study 1 headlines explicitly implicate social media in the misinformation problem.

6 Study 3: Why Does Misinformation Coverage Increase Media Trust?

Across two experiments, news coverage of misinformation (operationalized both with real-world news headlines and with a more general cue designed to increase the salience of the coverage) raises the public's trust in mainstream news, and in particular print news. Study 3 is an exploratory study investigating potential mechanisms for this effect, including the possibility that when people are concerned about misinformation, they place more value on adherence to professional journalistic norms.

People draw on a wide range of considerations when deciding how much to trust a particular news source. Existing attempts to identify some of these considerations have focused on aspects like completeness, accuracy, and fairness (Kohring and Matthes 2007; Prochazka and Schweiger 2019). However, in a series of interviews about media trust, Toff et al. (2021) find that people rarely spontaneously invoke the importance of editorial practices and professional norms. Rather, their explanations tend to focus more on familiarity and likeability, as well as appearance and style. These qualitative findings echo experimental work that shows people often instinctively rely on perceptions of media brands in evaluating trustworthiness (Urban and Schweiger 2014). In other words, considerations about journalistic practices (e.g. the extent to which they engage in fact-checking or source verification) are often not top-of-head when people are evaluating a source's trustworthiness.

Study 3 investigates whether exposure to news coverage of misinformation might alter these default dynamics. Increasing the salience of misinformation (and the perception that it is omnipresent) may lead people to place increased weight on news sources engaging in professional journalistic practices that could serve as bulwarks against misinformation, including checking and validating facts, relying on credible sources, and including relevant contextual information.

6.1 Study 3 Design

Study 3 was designed to elicit qualitative responses to media coverage of misinformation, with the goal of exploring how this news coverage might alter the relative importance of different dimensions of news trust. In total, 240 participants, recruited via Lucid, were randomly assigned to one of two conditions. Those in the treatment condition read headlines about misinformation, and those in the control condition read headlines about elections. The headlines were identical to those used in Study 2.

Then, participants were asked an open-ended question about media trust: "Please tell us what is most important to you when you are deciding what news sources to trust." The open-ended response data were classified into three nonexclusive categories developed prior to data collection, based on the dimensions identified by Knudsen et al. (2021) in their structural topic modeling of open-ended responses: truthfulness, adherence to professional journalistic norms, and (lack of) bias.[8]

---

[8] The "adherence to professional journalistic norms" category combines both the "thoroughness and professionalism" and "independence and objectivity" categories proposed by Knudsen et al. (2021).

Answers in the "truthfulness" category mentioned the importance of correctly and honestly reporting events and/or avoiding misinformation and fake news. It does not include explicit mentions of "accuracy," which were coded as falling into the "journalistic values" category. Examples of answers in the "truthfulness" category are as follows:

- Speaks the truth doesn't lie about things to benefit themselves
- If I am following a story I want the whole story and the truth...
- if it doesn't look like it's fake.
- That they're honest
- Facts and truth

Those in the "adherence to professional journalistic norms" category included comments about verifying sources, presenting the full set of facts, checking and validating sources, gatekeeping, and professional judgment. Examples in this category are as follows:

- That they have researched the story
- Proven track record of credibility.
- expert analysts, highly trained journalists, ethics and integrity
- to report all news fully and enable reader to easily fact check
- That they check their sources

Finally, the third category encompassed any mention of bias and/or objectivity, including mentions of explicit partisan slant as well as too much "opinion" being interjected into the news. Examples in this category are as follows:

- whether or not the articles appears to be biased or not
- want to know the facts not someone else's opinion
- Are they biased? Are they too far to the left or right? Are they pro-Trump?
- Bias. Do they take a stand and report opinions or do they report facts and let you form your own opinion.
- Sources that provide facts over opinions. Sources that do not suggest how I must digest the news.

The categories were not mutually exclusive, and 14% of responses were coded as falling into multiple categories. For example, the following response was coded as referencing all three categories: "Whether or not that source has published misinformation before, who is writing the story, and what political party or leanings, that source has."

Table 10 Effect of misinformation cue on references to different dimensions of trust.

	(Lack of) Bias		Truth		Journalistic values	
Misinformation headlines	−0.099*	(0.050)	−0.061	(0.044)	0.13*	(0.064)
Constant	0.33***	(0.080)	0.23**	(0.070)	0.32**	(0.10)
Observations	240		240		240	
Adjusted R^2	0.012		0.004		0.013	

Standard errors in parentheses

* $p < 0.05$, ** $p < 0.01$, *** $p < 0.001$

6.2 Study 3 Results

Two coders coded each of the open-ended responses. The intercoder reliability was at acceptable levels (truth: α=.72, values: α=.74, bias: α=.82,).[9]

In total, 58% of respondents who saw the misinformation headlines discussed some aspect of journalistic norms in their response, compared to 45% of respondents who saw the election headlines (p=.041). Exposure to the misinformation headlines also decreased references to bias: bias was mentioned by 23% of people in the election headlines group, but only 14% of those in the misinformation headlines group (p=.048). The groups were equally likely to reference truthfulness.

Table 10 shows the results of exposure to misinformation headlines (as compared to election headlines) on the likelihood of referencing the three different dimensions of credibility: (lack of) bias, truthfulness, and adherence to journalistic values.

Study 3 was designed to be exploratory rather than confirmatory, and it is important to emphasize that the survey employs a relatively small convenience sample. However, the results provide suggestive initial evidence that invoking misinformation might increase the salience of journalistic norms, and decrease the salience of perceived bias. These patterns demonstrate a potential mechanism for the effects observed in Studies 1 and 2: when people read headlines about misinformation, they are more likely to evaluate the trustworthiness of news sources based on how well those news sources are able to safeguard against the spreading of misinformation. And often, these safeguards take the

---

[9] In total, 65% of respondents answered in a way that fell into one of the three categories. Of the 35% who did not, the plurality wrote nothing or nonanswers (e.g. "good").

form of adherence to professional reporting standards like source verification, transparency, and training. People may thus see traditional print news, with its long history and emphasis on professional journalistic norms, as a bastion against the threat of misinformation.

Other research similarly suggests that encouraging audiences to consider reporting standards can improve trust. Participants who read a news article that included contextual information highlighting the journalistic process (e.g. information about the reporter and a "behind the story" section) perceived the issuing news organization as more credible (Curry and Stroud 2021). A similar study that randomly exposed participants to a "transparency box" with context about why a particular story was covered found similar effects on perceived credibility when the box was prominently featured (Masullo et al. 2022). Taken together, these studies reinforce that increasing the salience of journalistic norms is a potentially effective way of shifting trust.

The results of Study 3 are also consistent with how the mainstream media characterize the misinformation phenomenon. Not only do they consistently blame social media for "fake news," they often explicitly draw a contrast between the "Wild West" of social media and the high standards of traditional journalism. Emblematic of this coverage is a *Chicago Tribune* editorial decrying the dangers of social media and digital content, cited by Carlson (2020). Said the editors, "Rely on the mainstream news media. Professional journalists strive to report the news fairly – and take responsibility for the accuracy of their work." Study 3 suggests that these consistent efforts to paint mainstream media as the antidote to "fake news" may have been successful in shaping public opinion.

7 Conclusion

The four studies in this Element center on answering two questions that have critical implications for how the issue of misinformation informs public discourse. First, how do the media cover misinformation (and in particular, who do they blame for the problem)? Second, how does this coverage shape perceptions and opinions, including trust in media? I find evidence that news coverage of misinformation has substantially increased over the past eight years, and the media's consistent scapegoat of choice is social media. Consuming this coverage has two major effects: first, it increases estimates of how much misinformation is in the world; and second, it increases trust in traditional media (in particular, print) and decreases trust in news on social media.

Although answering these questions is the Element's primary focus, the results also make several other contributions to our understanding of media and public opinion, including providing insight into public interest in the "fake news" phenomenon and adding to the developing literature on how to understand and measure the concept of media trust in an increasingly fragmented information environment. This section discusses some of the implications of these findings, as well as outlining potential areas for future research.

7.1 Political Interest Predicts Engagement with Misinformation Coverage

While both Study 1 and Study 2 measure respondents' interest in news coverage of misinformation, they operationalize it in two different ways. In Study 1, participants were asked to explicitly state how interested they would be in reading a series of headlines, some of which were about misinformation. In Study 2, they were asked, "How closely have you been following news coverage of misinformation?" Despite these different approaches to measuring interest, the results were consistent between the two studies.

First, partisanship is not associated with interest: Democrats, Republicans, and Independents are all equally likely to engage with news about the misinformation phenomenon. This pattern is especially notable given the partisan asymmetry in exposure to *actual* misinformation: across multiple platforms and contexts, Republicans are more likely to encounter "fake news" than their Democratic counterparts (Guess, Nyhan and Reifler 2018; Eady et al. 2023; González-Bailón et al. 2023). Still, the results in this Element suggest that this increased exposure does not translate into increased (or decreased) interest in the topic more broadly. There are several potential reasons for this pattern. First, many people (regardless of their partisanship) struggle to identify false claims online, and so increased exposure does not necessarily suggest increased *awareness* of exposure. Second, it is possible that Republicans and Democrats differ in what aspects of the misinformation phenomenon interest them the most (e.g. the role of political elites, technological innovations, or fact-checking roundups). Future research could explore whether partisan interest varies along these topic dimensions.

Second, in both studies, age was negatively associated with interest in misinformation coverage: younger people are more engaged with this coverage than their older counterparts. This pattern is especially notable given research suggesting that older Americans are more susceptible to "fake news" (Gaillard et al. 2021). This difference could be partially explained by the close association between misinformation and social media – insofar as young people are heavier users of social media, they may also be more interested in news about misinformation on those platforms. Future qualitative research (e.g. interviews with news consumers) could explore some of the reasons for this difference.

Finally, political interest was a strong and consistent predictor of engagement with misinformation coverage, even more so than with political coverage more generally. This association is notable partly because it helps to explain some of the media's intense focus on the phenomenon. In an era when editorial decisions are increasingly informed by analytics (including clicks and social media performance), topics that generate consistent audience interest – especially among those already highly attuned to politics – are likely to receive more journalistic attention (Ferrucci 2020). This pattern can be exacerbated by several other factors. First, political interest correlates with education and income, which means that the politically engaged are also richer and tend to be richer, and thus more valuable for advertisers (Usher 2021). Insofar as misinformation is a topic of interest to these coveted readers, covering it more frequently can have direct financial benefits to publishers. Algorithms can also reinforce this feedback loop, as the politically interested are disproportionately exposed – and in turn engage with – particular types of content (Lin, Wang and Kim 2023). Misinformation deeply interests the minority of Americans who follow politics closely, and this interest incentivizes the media to continue its high levels of coverage. Finally, in an era when political coverage can be both polarizing and potentially alienating to partisans, the fact that headlines about misinformation and "fake news" are *not* seen as inherently more biased than other political coverage (see Section 3.4.1) makes it a potentially compelling topic for outlets seeking to increase engagement across partisan lines.

7.2 Attribution of Responsibility in Media Coverage of Misinformation

Analyzing *how* the media cover misinformation is necessary for understanding and theorizing about the potential effects of this coverage. Not only are the media a primary channel through which the public comes to understand complex issues (Lippmann 1922), they also shape who the public holds responsible for problems (Iyengar 1994; Kensicki 2004). The results of a content analysis show that media attention to this topic has grown, and the majority of articles either directly or indirectly attribute responsibility for misinformation to social media.

These results help to answer the question of why survey research consistently shows the substantial majority of Americans blame social media for misinformation (Seitz and Fingerhut 2021), despite the fact that in reality, most people encounter relatively little misinformation on social media (Guess, Nagler and

Tucker 2019). Other recent empirical work also indirectly confirms the public's perception that misinformation is rampant on social media. Lee, Gil de Zúñiga and Munger (2023) use panel data to show that while mainstream news use and social media news use are both associated with more actual exposure to "fake news," only social media use is associated with more *perceived* exposure to "fake news." In other words, social media users believe that they are exposed to more misinformation than non-social-media users, even though this pattern is not borne out by the data.

To what extent is the media's tendency to blame "fake news" and misinformation on social media objectively correct? While that empirical question is beyond the scope of this study, the answer matters for contextualizing these findings. Certainly, social media is an important vector for misinformation. However, attributing responsibility entirely to social media may have the unintentional negative effect of diverting attention away from the political actors and/or institutions who create that misinformation in the first place (Nyhan 2020). As McGregor and Kriess (2020) argue, rather than covering misinformation as a social media problem, media coverage should "pay more attention to the motivations, content, and drivers of mis- and disinformation."

Of course, the mainstream media sources analyzed in this Element (*The New York Times*, the *USA Today*, the Associated Press, and *The Washington Post* are not the public's only source of information about the issue of misinformation. While the content analysis presented in this Element gives a broad overview of how mainstream media covers misinformation (and most Americans have relatively centrist, mainstream media diets (Guess 2021)), the picture it paints is, of course, incomplete. The public's conception of the issue is also shaped by multiple other information sources, including television and social media, and these sources may frame the issue differently. Similar content analyses could examine how coverage varies by source factors like the partisanship of the news outlet as well as media type (e.g. television versus newspapers). This work would be especially important given the substantial literature demonstrating strong source effects in communication (Vraga and Bode 2017; Doherty and Hansen 2021). Expanding the content analysis to include other types of misinformation-related news coverage would also provide more nuanced insights. For example, Tsfati et al. (2020) point out that a great deal of mainstream news coverage of misinformation takes the form of fact-checks or debunking, and this type of article may have different effects than the more general media coverage of the phenomenon typified by the headlines in the experiment.

In addition, other types of media coverage may have different effects. For example, exposure to elites using "fake news" as an insult on Twitter may erode media trust (Van Duyn and Collier 2018). While this is not an example of media coverage per se, it does suggest that invoking the threat of misinformation does not always have positive effects on media trust. Future research should investigate the extent to which the effects of exposure to misinformation coverage on beliefs and attitudes depend on the source of the coverage (e.g. mainstream versus partisan news) and the type of coverage (e.g. focusing on social media versus foreign actors), as well as how this coverage is transmitted through social media (Anspach and Carlson 2020).

7.3 Misinformation Coverage Affects Estimates of Exposure Unequally Across Media Types

Public opinion and beliefs around the issue of misinformation profoundly affect both *whether* and *how* institutions and political actors respond to the problem. There is an enormous range of potential policy responses to misinformation, from government regulation and information literacy campaigns to inaction. What the public believes about the phenomenon – from how prevalent misinformation actually is to who is responsible for it – affects how public resources are allocated toward addressing the problem. While a surfeit of survey data shows a strong associations between perceptions of misinformation prevalence and concern over the issue, these data cannot tell us whether this association is driven by direct exposure to misinformation, or by something else. The experimental findings in this Element offer evidence for a *causal* impact of misinformation news coverage on perceptions of prevalence.

The results show that when people read about "fake news," they see it as more pervasive, as theories of agenda-setting would predict. This relationship suggests that the intensity and consistency of public concern over misinformation is driven in part by the media's focus on the issue. Of course, individuals' own interactions with misinformation (including on social media) also likely shape their perceptions of its prevalence, but these experiments show that the media can play an important causal role.

In addition, media coverage does not shape perceptions equally across source types. When people see headlines about misinformation (or are simply cued to consider news coverage of misinformation more broadly), their estimates of misinformation on social media *increase* but their estimates of misinformation in print media *decrease*. This finding, along with the results for media trust, suggests that people are able to make relatively sophisticated distinctions between the types of content that appear across different media sources. This insight is also supported by recent experimental work examining how the context in which an article is viewed affects perceptions of its credibility (Karlsen and

Aalberg 2023). Participants who were randomly assigned to see a news article on Facebook found it less trustworthy and more biased than those who saw the identical article on an online news site, suggesting that people have strong underlying priors about the likelihood that a piece of information on social media is credible. Media coverage may contribute to this belief by heightening the perception that "fake news" is rampant on social media.

7.4 Misinformation Coverage Increases Trust in Print Media

An important concern motivating this study was that just as exposure to "fake news" itself can lower trust in media (Ognyanova et al. 2020), exposure to news stories *about* misinformation might have a similar effect. The reasoning is intuitive: if a person comes to believe "fake news" is rampant, then how can they trust anything she sees? However, the results of these studies suggest that people are capable of drawing nuanced distinctions between different news sources. Across two experiments with different samples and different treatment operationalizations of media coverage, exposure to news about misinformation decreased trust in news on social media, but *increased* trust in print media (and, to a lesser degree, television). While this effect is not large, it is consistent across two studies, and runs counter to what many might intuitively expect to be the effects of increasing misinformation's salience.

These results also diverge from those of several other studies examining how *direct* exposure to misinformation (e.g. the "fake news" stories themselves) shapes media trust. In those studies, people who saw more "fake news" (measured both behaviorally and via self-reports) showed lower trust in media (Ognyanova et al. 2020; Lee, Gil de Zúñiga and Munger 2023). There are several (non mutually exclusive) potential explanations for this discrepancy. One possible explanation is that the negative association between direct misinformation exposure and decreased trust in media shown in observational studies does not actually reflect a causal relationship. Past research shows that exposure to misinformation tends to be concentrated among conservatives (Guess, Nagler and Tucker 2019; Rao, Morstatter and Lerman 2022), who consistently have much lower levels of media trust than their Democratic and Independent counterparts (Ladd and Podkul 2018). In other words, partisanship may be driving both lowered trust in media and exposure to misinformation.

A second explanation is that there is a fundamental difference between the type of misinformation circulating on social media (or elsewhere) and the *coverage* of this misinformation in news outlets. If misinformation circulating online is explicitly critical of the media and/or other institutions, then direct exposure to this may have deleterious effects on trust in a way that news coverage of the issue does not. And, indeed, disinformation campaigns – especially ones instigated by foreign actors – may be strategically designed to sow distrust (Wardle and Derakhshan 2017).

A third explanation, bolstered by the results of Study 3, is that when news coverage makes the issue of misinformation more salient, people place more weight on professional journalistic norms, and are less concerned about potential bias. Each of these is a meaningful finding in its own right. First, any intervention that makes people more carefully evaluate sources is worth further attention. As much as journalists might wish that people evaluated news sources based solely on the extent to which they verify their sources and fact-check, in reality this is rarely the case: instead, people tend to rely on heuristics like familiarity (Toff et al. 2021). The open-ended responses in Study 3 suggest that when faced with the threat of misinformation, people may stop and think more carefully about how journalistic norms and practices can protect against the dissemination of "fake news."

The fact that exposure to headlines about misinformation significantly decreases mentions of bias in the open-ended questions is also meaningful given that the public report high levels of concern about partisan bias in the news: 47% of Americans say that there is "so much bias in the news statement that it is difficult to sort out facts," and 26% of Americans say they can recall a specific instance of bias that made them trust a news source less (NORC 2016; Gallup 2017). Republicans are especially likely to report distrusting the media (Ladd 2011). Although the partisan asymmetry in actual exposure to "fake news" might suggest that the topic is especially susceptible to perceptions of partisan bias, the studies in this Element show little evidence of such concerns.

In the pretest, respondents (including Republicans) did not perceive headlines about "fake news" as having more partisan bias than headlines about elections more generally. In Studies 1 and 2, partisan bias was only rarely mentioned in the open-ended responses to the headlines. Finally, Study 2 showed exposure to the misinformation coverage cue increased media trust for both Republicans and Democrats alike. Study 3 offers a potential explanation for this lack of partisan difference: coverage of misinformation might actually *decrease* the extent to which concerns about bias influence media trust. This result makes sense in the context of the remarkable bipartisan nature of concern over misinformation: in a 2020 survey, equal numbers of Democrats and Republicans (85%) agreed that "outside groups or agents are actively trying to plant fake news stories on social media sites like Facebook, Twitter, and You-Tube" (Monmouth University 2020). Thus, especially as compared to divisive issues like immigration or race, both Republicans and Democrats can agree that misinformation is a problem.

7.5 The Importance of Better Operationalizations of Media Trust

This subsection discusses how this set of findings contribute to our understanding of media trust. First, it is important to note that the effect on trust is not merely an artifact of the particular headlines used in Study 1. While the treatment headlines in Study 1 explicitly mentioned the role of social media, the treatment in Study 2 did not. Instead, it increased the salience of "misinformation coverage" more generally, and an additional cue about "misinformation on social media" made no difference to the results. The fact that the differential effects on print versus social media trust replicate in Study 2 suggests that the public already strongly associates misinformation with social media. In other words, just as the content analysis would suggest, they have been "pre-treated" to draw a direct connection between misinformation and social media. Survey data support this inference: a 2020 Pew survey asked the 64% of respondents who said that social media has "a mostly negative effect on the way things are going in this country" to explain their answer in an open-ended format. The plurality mentioned misinformation: twice the size of the next-biggest category (Auxier 2020).

These patterns highlight the importance of employing more fine-grained measures of media trust, with the goal of better understanding how factors like social context and the information environment shape perceptions of journalistic reliability. Indeed, the difficulty of accurately measuring media trust is exacerbated by the fact that many people have very different conceptions of "news" – and, hence, very different standards for evaluating credibility (Edgerly and Vraga 2020; Schneiders 2023).

Currently, many media trust questions refer to the media as one monolithic entity. For example, the American National Election Study (ANES) asks, "How much of the time can you trust the media to report the news fairly?" The results of this study contribute to a growing literature that calls this type of measure into question by demonstrating that Americans are quite capable of distinguishing between types of media and evaluating them differently. Employing measures that specify different outlets or types of media allows for a more nuanced understanding of the factors that shape trust (Daniller et al. 2017; Ladd and Podkul 2018).

Finally, the fact that misinformation coverage *increases* trust in legacy media has implications that go well beyond the issue of misinformation. The advent of ChatGPT has already raised concerns that AI content creation tools could reduce media trust (Veiga 2023). Maybe the findings of this Element suggest another potential outcome: that consumers may see traditional media (including print news) as a bulwark against the perceived threats of new technology.

7.6 Unanswered Questions

This subsection takes on some of the major questions left unanswered by this Element. First, both the content analysis and the experiments omit an entire category of journalistic attention to misinformation: fact-checking. Over the past few decades, fact-checking enterprises, both within media organizations and external institutions, have grown enormously (Graves 2016). Fact-checking plays an important role in the information ecosystem: while few Americans directly visit fact-checking websites, fact-checkers' judgments influence both media coverage and elite behavior (Nyhan and Reifler 2015). A number of studies have examined the impact of exposure to fact-checks. While much of this research focuses on factors that make fact-checks more or less effective at reducing false beliefs (Young et al. 2018; Coppock et al. 2022), some also examines how exposure to fact-checks affects related attitudes like credibility and perceived bias (Bachmann and Valenzuela 2023; Shin 2023). For example, Bachmann and Valenzuela (2023) find that participants randomly assigned to view political fact-checks hold fewer misperceptions, but also express less trust in news.

What explains the difference between exposure to fact-checks and exposure to news about the misinformation phenomenon more broadly? One likely explanation is that fact-checks by definition take a stand on what is true versus false, which risks alienating some readers. Indeed, the negative impact of fact-check exposure on media trust was heightened when the fact-check debunks pro-attitudinal misinformation (Bachmann and Valenzuela 2023). In contrast, articles about the misinformation phenomenon more broadly are rarely focused on discrediting specific claims. For example, while a 2022 *New York Times* article headlined "On TikTok, Election Misinformation Thrives Ahead of Midterms" briefly mentions the *types* of misinformation circulating on the platform ("Health-related myths about Covid-19 vaccines and masks run rampant, as do rumors and falsehoods about diets, pediatric conditions and gender-affirming care for transgender people"), it does not explicitly discredit any specific claims in the way a fact-check would.

Still, the consistent negative effects of fact-check exposure on media trust suggest that future research should explore the boundary conditions of the findings in this Element. Clearly, not all media attention to misinformation increases trust. To what extent is this finding dependent on journalists *not* engaging in specific fact-checking? Given that misinformation is unlikely to disappear from the information ecosystem, how best to negotiate this tension will likely be an increasingly important normative and empirical question.

A second major question left unanswered by these studies (as well as most studies that seek to examine the factors that shape media trust) is exactly what media trust means for real-world behavior. How does increased (or decreased) trust shape behavior on a micro level (i.e. how people process and interpret individual stories) and the macro level (i.e. which news people choose to consume). Studies like Von Hohenberg and Guess (2022) that experimentally manipulate trust, then measure downstream attitudinal and behavioral consequences, are an important next step in understanding how changes in media trust affect larger patterns of news consumption and attitude formation.

7.7 News Coverage of Misinformation: Room for Optimism?

Recent estimates suggest that on average, that "fake news" comprises around 0.15% of Americans' media diet (Allen et al. 2020). This number stands in startling contrast to Americans' *perceptions* of how much of the information they see is false. This Element helps to solve the puzzle of why Americans are so convinced that misinformation is omnipresent despite its relatively low prevalence in their actual media diets: even people who have not directly encountered misinformation have likely seen media coverage of the issue. This exposure directly alters their perceptions not only of misinformation's ubiquity, but also of who is to blame: and for the most part, the media place this blame squarely on the shoulders of social media.

The rapid increase in news coverage of misinformation also raises important normative questions about its potential downstream effects on trust (Lazer et al. 2018; Tsfati et al. 2020). The studies in this Element offers some room for optimism, suggesting that misinformation coverage may not, as some have feared, erode political trust or trust in mainstream media. Rather, possibly because coverage of the topic leads people to place more value on professional journalistic norms, it can have the surprising effect of improving the reputation of legacy media.

Appendix for "How News Coverage of Misinformation Shapes Perceptions and Trust"

A Pretest: Partisanship and Perceptions of Bias

The pretest was designed to investigate (1) whether Republicans perceive articles about misinformation as more biased than articles about politics more generally and (2) whether the term "fake news" increases perceptions of bias. On average, Republicans said that 15% of the control headlines and 14% of the misinformation headlines were biased toward Democrats. Within the misinformation headlines, Republicans said that 20% of headlines that used the term "misinformation" were unbiased, compared to 23% of the "fake news" headlines. Democrats said that 29% of the headlines that used the term "misinformation" were unbiased, compared to 28% of the headlines using the term "fake news."

A.1 Additional Analyses

Table A.1 analyzes the question of partisan difference with an alternative approach. Each respondent received a 1 if they rated more of the misinformation articles as biased than the control articles (45% of respondents), and a 0 otherwise (55% of respondents). Table A.1 assesses the effect of (1) partisanship, (2) assignment to the "fake news" condition, and (3) an interaction between these two on the odds of perceiving the misinformation headlines as more biased than the control headlines.

Table A.1 Effect of partisanship and term on perceived bias

	Perceived bias	
Republican	1.55	(0.43)
"Fake news" condition	0.93	(0.26)
Republican × "fake news" condition	1.03	(0.41)
Observations	417	

Exponentiated coefficients; standard errors in parentheses
$^{*} p < 0.05$, $^{**} p < 0.01$, $^{***} p < 0.001$

B Study 1: Effects of Misinformation Coverage on Attitudes

B.1 Sample Size Considerations

A formal power analysis was not conducted prior to the experiment. The sample size was based on practical constraints as well as the goal of having around 1,000 respondents per comparison condition. This relatively large number was chosen partly so that it would be possible to conduct exploratory analyses of how effects vary between subgroups (e.g. political interest or education).

B.2 Additional Analyses

Table B.2 shows the distribution of self-reported media use in the sample.

Table B.2 Distribution of self-reported media use

	Never	Sometimes	Often
Facebook	36.4	37.7	36.3
Twitter	64.0	23.1	12.2
Local TV news	11.6	37.8	50.6
National TV news	37.5	36.7	25.8
Online news	17.0	44.2	38.8
Newspapers	35.9	44.3	19.9
FOX news	37.5	36.7	25.8
MSNBC	45.5	38.2	16.4

Table B.3 shows how the treatment affected respondents' estimates of how often the average person and they themselves were exposed to misinformation. The dependent variable is on a 1 (never) to 5 (every day) scale.

Table B.3 Effects on estimates of misinfo prevalence

	Average person		Self	
Misinfo headlines	0.17***	(0.040)	0.14**	(0.045)
Election headlines	−0.012	(0.041)	0.0045	(0.046)
Conspiratorial thinking	0.096***	(0.015)	0.094***	(0.016)
Political interest	0.26***	(0.023)	0.34***	(0.025)
Facebook	−0.071**	(0.023)	−0.023	(0.025)
Twitter	−0.055*	(0.026)	−0.062*	(0.029)

Table B.3 (*Cont.*)

	Average person		Self	
Local TV news	0.037	(0.026)	−0.017	(0.029)
Online news	0.14***	(0.025)	0.13***	(0.028)
Newspapers	0.0087	(0.025)	0.036	(0.027)
FOX News	0.0060	(0.022)	0.016	(0.025)
MSNBC	−0.040	(0.025)	−0.030	(0.028)
Constant	3.11***	(0.099)	2.63***	(0.11)
Observations	3222		3222	
Adjusted R^2	0.083		0.089	

Standard errors in parentheses

$^*\ p < 0.05, ^{**}\ p < 0.01, ^{***}\ p < 0.001$

Table B.4 shows how the treatment affected estimates of the percent of news across media outlets that is misinformation, and includes covariates.

Table B.4 Effects on estimates of percent of news that is misinfo across media types

	Newspapers		TV news		Social media news	
Misinfo headlines	−2.85**	(1.05)	−1.84	(1.12)	2.80**	(1.05)
Election headlines	−0.89	(1.06)	−1.57	(1.13)	0.46	(1.07)
Conspiratorial thinking	3.87***	(0.38)	3.63***	(0.40)	1.89***	(0.38)
Political interest	0.72	(0.59)	1.63**	(0.63)	1.08	(0.59)
Facebook	2.40***	(0.59)	2.93***	(0.63)	−2.10***	(0.60)
Twitter	3.09***	(0.68)	3.61***	(0.72)	−1.03	(0.68)
Local TV news	−3.21***	(0.69)	−5.81***	(0.73)	1.09	(0.69)
Online news	−2.93***	(0.66)	−1.49*	(0.70)	0.39	(0.66)
Newspapers	0.19	(0.64)	0.14	(0.68)	1.90**	(0.64)
FOX News	8.03***	(0.58)	7.09***	(0.62)	1.51**	(0.58)
MSNBC	−2.52***	(0.65)	−3.06***	(0.69)	0.64	(0.65)
Constant	27.3***	(2.58)	38.5***	(2.74)	49.5***	(2.58)
Observations	3155		3168		3197	
Adjusted R^2	0.119		0.107		0.023	

Standard errors in parentheses

$^*\ p < 0.05, ^{**}\ p < 0.01, ^{***}\ p < 0.001$

Appendix

Table B.5 shows the effect of viewing misinformation headlines on media trust, and includes covariates.

Table B.5 Effects on media trust

	Trust in media	
Treatments		
Misinfo headlines	0.071**	(0.027)
Election headlines	−0.0024	(0.027)
Attributes		
Conspiratorial thinking	−0.066***	(0.0097)
Political interest	0.050***	(0.015)
Media use		
Facebook	0.029	(0.015)
Twitter	0.031	(0.017)
Local TV news	0.28***	(0.018)
Online news	0.066***	(0.017)
Newspapers	0.076***	(0.016)
FOX News	−0.12***	(0.015)
MSNBC	0.20***	(0.017)
Constant	1.39***	(0.066)
Observations	3,201	
Adjusted R^2	0.212	

Standard errors in parentheses
$^*p < 0.05$, $^{**}p < 0.01$, $^{***}p < 0.001$

Table B.6 shows the effect of viewing misinformation headlines on internal efficacy and political trust, and includes covariates.

Table B.6 Effects on political trust and efficacy

	Political trust		Internal efficacy	
Misinfo headlines	0.0030	(0.0076)	−0.089**	(0.034)
Election headlines	−0.0062	(0.0077)	−0.054	(0.034)
Conspiratorial thinking	−0.041***	(0.0027)	−0.031*	(0.012)
Political interest	−0.0083	(0.0042)	0.56***	(0.019)

Table B.6 (*Cont.*)

	Political trust		Internal efficacy	
Facebook	0.015***	(0.0043)	−0.11***	(0.019)
Twitter	0.023***	(0.0049)	−0.028	(0.022)
Local TV news	0.0096	(0.0050)	−0.10***	(0.022)
Online news	−0.0034	(0.0048)	0.074***	(0.021)
Newspapers	0.022***	(0.0046)	0.11***	(0.021)
FOX News	0.019***	(0.0042)	0.012	(0.019)
MSNBC	0.027***	(0.0047)	−0.0021	(0.021)
Constant	0.31***	(0.019)	1.82***	(0.082)
Observations	3,157		3,228	
Adjusted R^2	0.111		0.284	

Standard errors in parentheses

* $p < 0.05$, ** $p < 0.01$, *** $p < 0.001$

C Study 2: Effect of Misinfo Coverge Salience on Media Trust

C.1 The TESS Platform

Time-sharing experiments for the social sciences (TESS) is a program through which researchers submit proposals for experiments. After review, TESS fields experiments on a representative sample of adults in the United States using NORC's AmeriSpeak Panel, a probability-based and representative survey platform.

The N for the study was not determined by the researcher, but rather by the constraints of the TESS Short Studies program (https://tessexperiments.org/info/ssp), of which this was a part. As per the website guidelines, "Successful proposals submitted to the SSP will be fielded on a general population sample of 1600 adults in the United States."

D Study 3: News Coverage of Misinformation and Dimensions of Media Trust

D.1 Inter-coder Reliability

All of the 240 open-ended responses were coded by two independent coders who were given the instructions below. The inter-coder reliability was at acceptable levels (values: $\alpha = .74$, bias: $\alpha = .82$, truth: $\alpha = .72$). In total, 65% of respondents answered in a way that fell into one of the three categories. Of the 35% who did not, the plurality wrote nothing or non-answers (e.g. "good").

Bias: This category includes answers that invoke concerns about bias or lack of objectivity. This includes any mention of bias or slant as well as concerns about too much "opinion."

Truthfulness: This category includes answers that discuss the importance of the truth and/or avoiding misinformation and fake news. It does not include mentions of "accuracy," which belong to the "professional journalistic values" category. It does include mentions of truth, truthfulness, honesty, misinformation, and fake news.

Professional journalistic values: This category includes practices associated with professional journalistic norms, including sources (using multiple sources, credibility of sources), checking and validating information, accuracy, professional judgment and research, integrity and credibility of brand/source, reputation, inclusion of all relevant information, and inclusion of facts and/or use of fact-checking.

E Survey Instruments

E.1 Study 1 Survey Instrument

Are you male or female?
- Male
- Female
- Prefer not to say

In what year were you born?

Do you agree or disagree with the following statements [strongly disagree, somewhat disagree, neither agree nor disagree, somewhat agree, strongly agree]
- Much of our lives are being controlled by plots hatched in secret.
- Even though we live in a democracy, a few people will always run things anyway.
- The people who really "run" the country are not known to voters.
- Big events like wars and the outcomes of elections are controlled by small groups of people who are working in secret.

How closely do you follow what's going on in government and public affairs?
- Very closely
- Somewhat closely

- Not that closely
- Not at all

People get news from many different sources. Please indicate how often you get news from the following sources [never, sometimes, often]:
- Facebook
- Twitter
- Fox News
- Local TV news
- MSNBC
- Online news websites
- Print newspaper

Different people prefer different types of news stories. We're interested in learning more about the types of news you prefer. Next, you will see six recent news headlines. Read each headline, then indicate how interesting you find the story and choose which of two statements best describes the story. If you're not sure, just give your best guess. Please pay close attention to the headlines, as you will be asked questions about them later on in the survey.

[Respondents are randomly assigned to either receive all six election headlines, or five misinformation headlines and one election headline. Each is followed by a question asking them to rate how interested they are in the headline, and a brief factual question about the headline's contents.]

Election headlines
Election Uncertainty Spurs Investors to Hedge
Campaigns Are Texting Voters Out of The Blue
Posting Political Signs in the Window Is Your Right - Isn't It?
Advertising War Already Started During Tough Election Season
After A Tough 2016, Many Pollsters Haven't Changed Anything
Wandering Voters Key to Presidential Race

Misinformation headlines
Fighting Misinformation on Social Media Has Proven Lucrative for Tech Groups
Facebook Will Now Fact-Check Photos, Videos as it Fights Misinformation
Fake News on Social Media Platforms is a New Kind of Cybersecurity Attack
How Can Students Learn to Distinguish Misinformation from Real News?
Google Announces Plan to Combat Spread of Fake News
(One headline inserted at random from the "Election Headlines" condition)

What thoughts came to mind when reading those headlines?
- [open-ended]

Overall, about what percentage of the news that appears in the following places do you think is misinformation? [0 – 100]
- Social media
- Newspapers
- Television news

About how frequently do you think the average person encounters political misinformation? This might be in the news, via social media, or in other ways.
- Every day
- A few times a week
- A few times a month
- A few times a year
- Rarely or never

And about how frequently do you think you personally encounter political misinformation?
- Every day
- A few times a week
- A few times a month
- A few times a year
- Rarely or never

Do you think the spread of inaccurate information on the Internet is:
- A very important problem
- A somewhat important problem
- A minor problem
- Not a problem

Do you agree or disagree with the following statements? [strongly disagree, somewhat disagree, neither agree nor disagree, somewhat agree, strongly agree]
- Sometimes, politics seem so complicated that a person like me can't really understand what's going on.
- I feel that I have a pretty good understanding of the important political issues debated by the government.
- I consider myself well-qualified to participate in politics.

How much, if at all, do you trust the information you get from...
- National news organizations
- Local news organizations
- Friends, family, and acquaintances
- Social networking sites, such as Facebook and Twitter

How much of the time do you think you can trust the news media to report the news fairly?
- Just about always
- Most of the time
- Some of the time
- Almost never

Do you agree or disagree with the following statements? [strongly disagree, somewhat disagree, neither agree nor disagree, somewhat agree, strongly agree]
- Most politicians are trustworthy.
- Politicians in the US do not deserve much respect.
- Politicians generally have good intentions.

In general, how often can you trust the government in Washington to do what is right?
- All of the time
- Most of the time
- Some of the time
- None of the time

Please rank the following institutions on a scale from 0 to 100. Zero means you feel very unfavorable toward them, and 100 means very you feel very favorable. Fifty means you do not feel favorable or unfavorable.
- The news media
- Facebook
- Congress
- The Republican party
- The Democratic party

Generally speaking, do you think of yourself as a:
- Democrat
- Republican
- Independent

- Another party
- No preference

[if no party in previous question] Would you say that you are closer to the Democratic party or the Republican party?
- Democrat
- Republican

What is the highest degree or level of school you have completed?
- Did not graduate from high school
- High school diploma or the equivalent (GED)
- Some college
- Associate degree
- Bachelor's degree
- Master's degree
- Professional or doctorate degree

Earlier, you read a series of headlines. This question is about those headlines. Were some of the headlines you saw earlier specifically about the issue of misinformation?
- Yes
- No

E.2 Study 2 Survey Instrument

Respondents were part of the NORC panel and party identification was collected during a previous wave of the panel.

How closely do you follow politics and government affairs?
- Very closely
- Somewhat closely
- Not that closely
- Not at all

People get news from many different sources. Please indicate how often you get news from the following sources [never, hardly ever, sometimes, often]
- Facebook
- Twitter
- Print newspaper
- Local TV news

- Fox News
- MSNBC
- Online news websites

[Treatment group receives this question BEFORE the media trust and misinformation estimate questions; Control group receives it AFTER] Lately, there have been a lot of news stories about the spread of political misinformation. How closely are you following news about this issue?
- Very closely
- Somewhat closely
- Not that closely
- Not at all closely

Overall, about what percentage of the news that appears in the following places do you think is misinformation? [0 – 100]
- Social media
- Newspapers
- Television

How much do you trust news from the following sources? [1 – 5 scale]
- Local newspapers
- National newspapers
- Facebook
- Twitter
- Network TV news
- Local TV news

E.3 Study 3 Survey Instrument

In what year were you born?

How closely do you follow what's going on in government and public affairs?
- Very closely
- Somewhat closely
- Not that closely
- Not at all

People get news from many different sources. Please indicate how often you get news from the following sources [never, sometimes, often]:
- Facebook
- Twitter

- Fox News
- Local TV news
- MSNBC
- Online news websites
- Print newspaper

Different people prefer different types of news stories. We're interested in learning more about the types of news you prefer. Next, you will see six recent news headlines. Read each headline, then indicate how interesting you find the story and choose which of two statements best describes the story. If you're not sure, just give your best guess. Please pay close attention to the headlines, as you will be asked questions about them later on in the survey.

[Respondents are randomly assigned to either receive all six election headlines, or five misinformation headlines and one election headline. Each is followed by a question asking them to rate how interested they are in the headline, and a brief factual question about the headline's contents.]

Election headlines
Election Uncertainty Spurs Investors to Hedge
Campaigns Are Texting Voters Out of The Blue
Posting Political Signs in the Window Is Your Right – Isn't It?
Advertising War Already Started During Tough Election Season
After A Tough 2016, Many Pollsters Haven't Changed Anything
Wandering Voters Key to Presidential Race

Misinformation headlines
Fighting Misinformation on Social Media Has Proven Lucrative for Tech
    Groups
Facebook Will Now Fact-Check Photos, Videos as it Fights Misinformation
Fake News on Social Media Platforms is a New Kind of Cybersecurity Attack
How Can Students Learn to Distinguish Misinformation from Real News?
Google Announces Plan to Combat Spread of Fake News
(One headline inserted at random from the "Election Headlines" condition)

Please tell us what is most important to you when you are deciding what news sources to trust.
- [open-ended]

Overall, about what percentage of the news that appears in the following places do you think is misinformation? [0 – 100]
- Social media
- Newspapers
- Television news

About how frequently do you think the average person encounters political misinformation? This might be in the news, via social media, or in other ways.
- Every day
- A few times a week
- A few times a month
- A few times a year
- Rarely or never

And about how frequently do you think you personally encounter political misinformation?
- Every day
- A few times a week
- A few times a month
- A few times a year
- Rarely or never

Do you think the spread of inaccurate information on the Internet is:
- A very important problem
- A somewhat important problem
- A minor problem
- Not a problem

References

Allcott, Hunt and Matthew Gentzkow. 2017. "Social media and fake news in the 2016 election." *Journal of Economic Perspectives* 31(2):211–236.

Allen, Jennifer, Baird Howland, Markus Mobius, David Rothschild and Duncan J. Watts. 2020. "Evaluating the fake news problem at the scale of the information ecosystem." *Science Advances* 6(14):eaay3539.

Altay, Sacha and Alberto Acerbi. 2023. "People believe misinformation is a threat because they assume others are gullible." *New Media & Society*: 14614448231153379.

Amazeen, Michelle A. 2020. "Journalistic interventions: The structural factors affecting the global emergence of fact-checking." *Journalism* 21(1):95–111.

Anspach, Nicolas M. and Taylor N. Carlson. 2020. "What to believe? Social media commentary and belief in misinformation." *Political Behavior* 42(3):697–718.

Arceneaux, Kevin and Martin Johnson. 2013. *Changing minds or changing channels? Partisan news in an age of choice.* University of Chicago Press.

Auxier, Brooke. 2020. "64 percent of Americans say social media have a mostly negative effect on the way things are going in the U.S. today." *Pew Research Center. www.pewresearch.org/fact-tank/2020/10/15/64-of-americans-say-social-media-have-a-mostly-negative-effect-on-the-way-things-are-going-in-the-u-s-today/.*

Bachmann, Ingrid and Sebastián Valenzuela. 2023. "Studying the downstream effects of fact-checking on social media: Experiments on correction formats, belief accuracy, and media trust." *Social Media+ Society* 9(2):20563051231179694.

Bacon Jr, Perry and Dhrumil Mehta. 2018. "Very few voters actually read Trump's tweets." *FiveThirtyEight. https://fivethirtyeight.com/features/very-few-voters-actually-read-trumps-tweets/.*

Ball, Philip and Amy Maxmen. 2020. "The epic battle against coronavirus misinformation and conspiracy theories." *Nature* 581(7809):371–375.

Barari, Soubhik, Christopher Lucas and Kevin Munger. 2021. "Political deepfakes are as credible as other fake media and (sometimes) real media." *OSF Preprints* 13.

Barthel, Michael, Amy Mitchell and Jesse Holcomb. 2016. Many Americans Believe Fake News Is Sowing Confusion. Technical report Pew Research Center.

Bennett, W. Lance and Steven Livingston. 2018. "The disinformation order: Disruptive communication and the decline of democratic institutions." *European Journal of Communication* 33(2):122–139.

Berinsky, Adam J. 2017. "Rumors and health care reform: Experiments in political misinformation." *British Journal of Political Science* 47(2): 241–262.

Berlinski, Nicolas, Margaret Doyle, Andrew M. Guess, et al. 2023. "The effects of unsubstantiated claims of voter fraud on confidence in elections." *Journal of Experimental Political Science* 10(1):34–49.

Bode, Leticia, Emily K. Vraga and Sonya Troller-Renfree. 2017. "Skipping politics: Measuring avoidance of political content in social media." *Research & Politics* 4(2):2053168017702990.

Brenan, Megan. 2022. "Americans' trust in media remains near record low." *Gallup. https://news.gallup.com/poll/403166/americans-trust-media-remains-near-record-low.aspx.*

Brewer, Paul R. and Kimberly Gross. 2005. "Values, framing, and citizens' thoughts about policy issues: Effects on content and quantity." *Political Psychology* 26(6):929–948.

Britzky, Haley. 2017. "Everything Trump has labeled as fake news." *Axios. www.axios.com/everything-trump-has-called-fake-news-1513303959-6603 329e-46b5-44ea-b6be-70d0b3bdb0ca.html.*

Carlson, Matt. 2020. "Fake news as an informational moral panic: The symbolic deviancy of social media during the 2016 US presidential election." *Information, Communication & Society* 23(3):374–388.

CBSNews. 2018. "Lesley Stahl: Trump admitted mission to discredit press." *cbsnews.com. www.cbsnews.com/news/lesley-stahl-donald-trump-said-attacking-press-to-discredit-negative-stories/.*

Clayton, Katherine, Spencer Blair, Jonathan A. Busam, Samuel Forstner, John Glance, Guy Green, Anna Kawata et al. "Real solutions for fake news? Measuring the effectiveness of general warnings and fact-check tags in reducing belief in false stories on social media." *Political Behavior* 42(2020):1073–1095.

Coppock, Alexander, Kimberly Gross, Ethan Porter, Emily Thorson, and Thomas J. Wood. "Conceptual Replication of Four Key Findings about Factual Corrections and Misinformation during the 2020 US Election: Evidence from Panel-Survey Experiments." *British Journal of Political Science* 53, no. 4 (2023):1328–1341.

Coppock, Alexander and Oliver A. McClellan. 2019. "Validating the demographic, political, psychological, and experimental results obtained from a new source of online survey respondents." *Research & Politics* 6(1):1073–1095.

Curry, Alexander L. and Natalie Jomini Stroud. 2021. "The effects of journalistic transparency on credibility assessments and engagement intentions." *Journalism* 22(4):901–918.

Daniller, Andrew, Douglas Allen, Ashley Tallevi and Diana C. Mutz. 2017. "Measuring trust in the press in a changing media environment." *Communication Methods and Measures* 11(1):76–85.

Diaz, Andrea. 2018. "'Misinformation' is crowned Dictionary.com's word of the year." *CNN. www.cnn.com/2018/11/26/us/misinformation-dictionary-word-of-the-year-2018-trnd/index.html.*

Doherty, David and Kathryn Hansen. 2021. "Partisan identities and interpretations of economic data." *Politics, Groups, and Identities* 10(4):705–714

Eady, Gregory, Tom Paskhalis, Jan Zilinsky, et al. 2023. "Exposure to the Russian Internet Research Agency foreign influence campaign on Twitter in the 2016 US election and its relationship to attitudes and voting behavior." *Nature Communications* 14(1):62.

Edgerly, Stephanie and Emily K. Vraga. 2020. "Deciding what's news: Newsness as an audience concept for the hybrid media environment." *Journalism & Mass Communication Quarterly* 97(2):416–434.

Egelhofer, Jana Laura, Loes Aaldering, Jakob-Moritz Eberl, Sebastian Galyga and Sophie Lecheler. 2020. "From novelty to normalization? How journalists use the term 'fake news' in their reporting." *Journalism Studies* 21(10):1323–1343.

Egelhofer, Jana Laura and Sophie Lecheler. 2019. "Fake news as a two-dimensional phenomenon: A framework and research agenda." *Annals of the International Communication Association* 43(2):97–116.

Farhall, Kate, Andrea Carson, Scott Wright, Andrew Gibbons and William Lukamto. 2019. "Political elites' use of fake news discourse across communications platforms." *International Journal of Communication* 13:23.

Farkas, Johan. 2023. "News on fake news: Logics of media discourses on disinformation." *Journal of Language and Politics* 22(1):1–21.

Ferracioli, Paulo, Andressa Butture Kniess and Francisco Paulo Jamil Marques. 2022. "The watchdog role of fact-checkers in different media systems." *Digital Journalism* 10(5):717–737.

Ferrucci, Patrick. 2020. "It is in the numbers: How market orientation impacts journalists' use of news metrics." *Journalism* 21(2):244–261.

Funke, Daniel. 2017. "Should we stop saying 'fake news'?" *Poynter. www.poynter.org/fact-checking/2017/should-we-stop-saying-fake-news/.*

Funke, Daniel. 2018*a*. "'Misinformation' is Dictionary.com's word of the year." *Poynter*. *www.poynter.org/fact-checking/2018/misinformation-is-dictionary-coms-word-of-the-year/*.

Funke, Daniel. 2018*b*. "Reporters: Stop calling everything fake news." *Poynter*. *www.poynter.org/fact-checking/2018/reporters-stop-calling-everything-fake-news/*.

Gabielkov, Maksym, A. Ramachandran, A. Chaintreau and A. Legout. 2016. "Social clicks: What and who gets read on Twitter?" *ACM SIGMETRICS Performance Evaluation Review* 44(1):179–192.

Gaillard, Stefan, Zoril A. Oláh, Stephan Venmans and Michael Burke. 2021. "Countering the cognitive, linguistic, and psychological underpinnings behind susceptibility to fake news: A review of current literature with special focus on the role of age and digital literacy." *Frontiers in Communication* 6:661801.

Gallup. 2017. American Views: Trust, Media, and Democracy. Technical report Knight Foundation.

Gallup. 2018. "Americans' view of misinformation in the news and how to counter it." *https://knightfoundation.org/reports/americans-views-of-misinformation-in-the-news-and-how-to-counteract-it/*.

González-Bailón, Sandra, David Lazer, Pablo Barberá, et al. 2023. "Asymmetric ideological segregation in exposure to political news on Facebook." *Science* 381(6656):392–398.

Gottfried, Jeffrey, Amy Mitchell, Mark Jurkowitz and Jacob Liedke. 2022. Journalists Sense Turmoil in Their Industry Amid Continued Passion for Their Work. Technical report Pew Research Center.

Graves, Lucas. 2016. *Deciding what's true: The rise of political fact-checking in American journalism*. Columbia University Press.

Graves, Lucas, Brendan Nyhan and Jason Reifler. 2016. "Understanding innovations in journalistic practice: A field experiment examining motivations for fact-checking." *Journal of Communication* 66(1):102–138.

Grinberg, Nir, Kenneth Joseph, Lisa Friedland, Briony Swire-Thompson and David Lazer. 2019. "Fake news on Twitter during the 2016 US presidential election." *Science* 363(6425):374–378.

Guess, Andrew, Brendan Nyhan and Jason Reifler. 2018. "Selective exposure to misinformation: Evidence from the consumption of fake news during the 2016 US presidential campaign." European Research Council.

Guess, Andrew, Jonathan Nagler and Joshua Tucker. 2019. "Less than you think: Prevalence and predictors of fake news dissemination on Facebook." *Science Advances* 5(1):eaau4586.

Guess, Andrew M. 2021. "(Almost) Everything in moderation: New evidence on Americans' online media diets." *American Journal of Political Science* 65(4):1007–1022.

Guess, Andrew M., Brendan Nyhan and Jason Reifler. 2020. "Exposure to untrustworthy websites in the 2016 US election." *Nature Human Behaviour* 4(5):472–480.

Guess, Andrew M., Dominique Lockett, Benjamin Lyons, et al. 2020. " 'Fake news' may have limited effects beyond increasing beliefs in false claims." *Harvard Kennedy School Misinformation Review* 1(1).

Guess, Andrew M. and Kevin Munger. 2023. "Digital literacy and online political behavior." *Political Science Research and Methods* 11(1): 110–128.

Guynn, Jessica. 2018. "Clock ticking for Facebook to halt election meddling." *USA Today. www.usatoday.com/story/tech/2018/01/22/facebook-tries-wipe-out-election-meddling-before-2018-midterms/1055710001/.*

Habgood-Coote, Joshua. 2018. "Why we should stop using the term 'fake news'." *Newsweek. www.newsweek.com/why-we-should-stop-using-term-fake-news-opinion-1047951.*

Hasen, Richard. 2022. "How to keep the rising tide of fake news from drowning our Democracy." *New York Times*, March 7, 2022, *www.nytimes.com/2022/03/07/opinion/cheap-speech-fake-news-democracy.html.*

Invernizzi, Giovanna M. and Ahmed Ezzeldin Mohamed. 2023. "Trust nobody: How voters react to conspiracy theories." *Journal of Experimental Political Science* 10(2):201–208.

Italie, Leanne. 2018. "'Misinformation' is Dictionary.com's word of the year." *NBC10 Philadelphia. www.nbcphiladelphia.com/news/local/Misin-formation-Is-Dictionarycom-Word-of-the-Year-501237371.html.*

Iyengar, Shanto. 1994. *Is anyone responsible?: How television frames political issues*. University of Chicago Press.

Jacobs, Emily. 2018. "Dictionary.com picks 'misinformation' as word of the year, cites Trump." *New York Post. https://nypost.com/2018/11/26/diction-ary-com-picks-misinformation-as-word-of-the-year-cites-trump/.*

Jamieson, Kathleen Hall. 2020. *Cyberwar: How Russian hackers and trolls helped elect a president: What we don't, can't, and do know*. Oxford University Press.

Jerit, Jennifer and Yangzi Zhao. 2020. "Political misinformation." *Annual Review of Political Science* 23:77–94.

Jones-Jang, S. Mo, Dam Hee Kim and Kate Kenski. 2021. "Perceptions of mis- or disinformation exposure predict political cynicism: Evidence from a two-wave survey during the 2018 US midterm elections." *New Media & Society* 23(10):3105–3125.

Kahneman, Daniel. 2011. *Thinking, fast and slow*. Macmillan.

Karlsen, Rune and Toril Aalberg. 2023. "Social media and trust in news: An experimental study of the effect of Facebook on news story credibility." *Digital Journalism* 11(1):144–160.

Kelly, Makena. 2022. "New algorithm bill could force Facebook to change how the news feed works." *The Verge*. *www.theverge.com/2022/2/10/22927472/klobuchar-lummis-algorithm-bill-section-230-misinformation-teenager-mental-health*.

Kensicki, Linda Jean. 2004. "No cure for what ails us: The media-constructed disconnect between societal problems and possible solutions." *Journalism & Mass Communication Quarterly* 81(1):53–73.

Knudsen, Erik, Stefan Dahlberg, Magnus H. Iversen, Mikael P. Johannesson and Silje Nygaard. 2021. "How the public understands news media trust: An open-ended approach." *Journalism* 23(11):2347–2363.

Kohring, Matthias and Jörg Matthes. 2007. "Trust in news media: Development and validation of a multidimensional scale." *Communication Research* 34(2):231–252.

Krupnikov, Yanna and John Barry Ryan. 2022. *The other divide*. Cambridge University Press.

Kurtzleben, Danielle. 2017. "With 'fake news,' Trump moves from alternative facts to alternative language." *NPR News*. *www.npr.org/2017/02/17/515630467/with-fake-news-trump-moves-from-alternative-facts-to-alternative-language*.

Ladd, Jonathan M. 2011. *Why Americans hate the media and how it matters*. Princeton University Press.

Ladd, Jonathan M. and Alexander R. Podkul. 2018. "Distrust of the news media as a symptom and a further cause of partisan polarization." In Travis Ridout (ed.), *New directions in media and politics*. Routledge pp. 54–79.

Landis, J. Richard and Gary G. Koch. 1977. "The measurement of observer agreement for categorical data." *Biometrics* 33(1):159–174.

Lazer, David M.J., Matthew A. Baum, Yochai Benkler, et al. 2018. "The science of fake news." *Science* 359(6380):1094–1096.

Lee, Sangwon, Homero Gil de Zúñiga and Kevin Munger. 2023. "Antecedents and consequences of fake news exposure: A two-panel study on how news use and different indicators of fake news exposure affect media trust." *Human Communication Research* 49(4):408–420.

Levendusky, Matthew and Neil Malhotra. 2016. "Does media coverage of partisan polarization affect political attitdes?" *Political Communication* 33(2):283–301.

Lima, Gabriel, Jiyoung Han and Meeyoung Cha. 2022. "Others are to blame: Whom people consider responsible for online misinformation." *Proceedings of the ACM on Human-Computer Interaction* 6(CSCW1):1–25.

Lin, Han, Yi Wang and Yonghwan Kim. 2023. "The rich get richer and the poor get poorer? The effect of news recommendation algorithms in exacerbating inequalities in news engagement and social capital." *New Media & Society* 14614448231168572.

Lippmann, Walter. 1922. *Public opinion*. Transaction Publishers.

Lischka, Juliane A. 2019. "A badge of honor? How the New York Times discredits president Trump's fake news accusations." *Journalism Studies* 20(2):287–304.

Lowry, Dennis T., Tarn Ching Josephine Nio and Dennis W. Leitner. 2003. "Setting the public fear agenda: A longitudinal analysis of network TV crime reporting, public perceptions of crime, and FBI crime statistics." *Journal of Communication* 53(1):61–73.

MacFarquhar, Neil. 2017. "With big red stamp, Russia singles out what it calls 'fake' news." *New York Times. www.nytimes.com/2017/02/22/world/europe/ russia-fake-news-media-foreign-ministry-.html*.

Marsh, Michael and James Tilley. 2010. "The attribution of credit and blame to governments and its impact on vote choice." *British Journal of Political Science* 40(1):115–134.

Masullo, Gina M., Alexander L. Curry, Kelsey N. Whipple and Caroline Murray. 2022. "The story behind the story: Examining transparency about the journalistic process and news outlet credibility." *Journalism Practice* 16(7):1287–1305.

McClure Haughey, Melinda, Meena Devii Muralikumar, Cameron A. Wood and Kate Starbird. 2020. "On the misinformation beat: Understanding the work of investigative journalists reporting on problematic information online." *Proceedings of the ACM on Human-Computer Interaction* 4(CSCW2):1–22.

McCombs, Maxwell. 2005. "A look at agenda-setting: Past, present and future." *Journalism Studies* 6(4):543–557.

McCombs, Maxwell E. and Donald L. Shaw. 1972. "The agenda-setting function of mass media." *Public Opinion Quarterly* 36(2):176–187.

McGlynn, Joseph and Matthew S. McGlone. 2019. "Desire or disease? Framing obesity to influence attributions of responsibility and policy support." *Health Communication* 34(7):689–701.

McGregor, Shannon and Daniel Kriess. 2020. "Slate." *Americans Are Too Worried About Political Misinformation. https://slate.com/technology/2020/10/misinformation-social-media-election-research-fear.html.*

Meeks, Lindsey. 2020. "Defining the enemy: How Donald Trump frames the news media." *Journalism & Mass Communication Quarterly* 97(1):211–234.

Meyer, Robinson. 2018. "Why it's okay to call it fake news." *The Atlantic. www.theatlantic.com/technology/archive/2018/03/why-its-okay-to-say-fake-news/555215/.*

Montgomery, Jacob M., Brendan Nyhan and Michelle Torres. 2018. "How conditioning on posttreatment variables can ruin your experiment and what to do about it." *American Journal of Political Science* 62(3):760–775.

Munger, Kevin. 2020. "All the news that's fit to click: The economics of clickbait media." *Political Communication* 37(3):376–397.

Murray, Patrick. 2018. Monmouth Polling Institute. Technical report Monmouth University.

Nelson, Jacob L. 2021. "The next media regime: The pursuit of 'audience engagement' in journalism." *Journalism* 22(9):2350–2367.

Newman, Nic. 2018. "Reuters institute digital news report 2018." Reuters Institute for the Study of Journalism.

NORC. 2016. A New Understanding: What Makes People Trust and Rely on News. Technical report American Press Institute.

NORC. 2018. Americans and the News Media. Technical report American Press Institute.

Nyhan, Brendan. 2010. "Why the "death panel" myth wouldn't die: Misinformation in the health care reform debate." *The Forum* 8(1).

Nyhan, Brendan. 2020. "Facts and myths about Misperceptions." *Journal of Economic Perspectives* 34(3):220–236.

Nyhan, Brendan and Jason Reifler. 2015. "The effect of fact-checking on elites: A field experiment on US state legislators." *American Journal of Political Science* 59(3):628–640.

Ognyanova, Katherine, David Lazer, Ronald E Robertson and Christo Wilson. 2020. "Misinformation in action: Fake news exposure is linked to lower trust in media, higher trust in government when your side is in power." *Harvard Kennedy School Misinformation Review. https://misinforeview .hks.harvard.edu/article/misinformation-in-action-fake-news-exposure-is-linked-to-lower-trust-in-media-higher-trust-in-government-when-your-side-is-in-power/.*

Ott, Brian L. 2017. "The age of Twitter: Donald J. Trump and the politics of debasement." *Critical Studies in Media Communication* 34(1):59–68.

Pasek, Josh, Gaurav Sood and Jon A. Krosnick. 2015. "Misinformed about the affordable care act? Leveraging certainty to assess the prevalence of misperceptions." *Journal of Communication* 65(4):660–673.

Pingree, Raymond J., Megan Hill and Douglas M. McLeod. 2013. "Distinguishing effects of game framing and journalistic adjudication on cynicism and epistemic political efficacy." *Communication Research* 40(2): 193–214.

Porter, Ethan, Yamil Velez and Thomas J. Wood. 2023. "Correcting COVID-19 vaccine misinformation in 10 countries." *Royal Society Open Science* 10(3):221097.

Prochazka, Fabian and Wolfgang Schweiger. 2019. "How to measure generalized trust in news media? An adaptation and test of scales." *Communication Methods and Measures* 13(1):26–42.

Rao, Ashwin, Fred Morstatter and Kristina Lerman. 2022. "Partisan asymmetries in exposure to misinformation." *Scientific Reports* 12(1):15671.

Riddle, Karyn. 2010. "Always on my mind: Exploring how frequent, recent, and vivid television portrayals are used in the formation of social reality judgments." *Media Psychology* 13(2):155–179.

Romer, Daniel, Kathleen Hall Jamieson and Sean Aday. 2003. "Television news and the cultivation of fear of crime." *Journal of Communication* 53(1):88–104.

Ross, Andrew S and Damian J Rivers. 2018. "Discursive deflection: Accusation of "fake news" and the spread of mis-and disinformation in the tweets of president Trump." *Social Media+ Society* 4(2):2056305118776010.

Schneiders, Pascal. 2023. "News from the user's perspective: With naivety to validity." *Digital Journalism*: 1–22.

Searles, Kathleen and Jessica T. Feezell. 2023. "Scrollability: A new digital news affordance." *Political Communication* 40(5):670–675.

Seitz, Amanda. 2020. "Virus misinformation flourishes in online protest groups." *Associated Press*. *https://apnews.com/article/donald-trump-us-news-ap-top-news-politics-virus-outbreak-5862a9201c7b1bea62069a9c5e5fbb1c.*

Seitz, Amanda and Hannah Fingerhut. 2021. "Americans agree misinformation is a problem, poll shows." *PBS NewsHour. www.pbs.org/newshour/nation/americans-agree-misinformation-is-a-problem-poll-shows.*

Shin, Hwayong. 2023. "Building credibility in polarized environments: Evidence from fact-checking"

Stephens, Bret. 2023. "How to destroy (what's left of) the mainstream media's credibility." *New York Times*, February 9, 2023. *www.nytimes.com/2023/02/09/opinion/mainstream-media-credibility-objectivity-journalism.html.*

Strauss, Natalie. 2018. "Word of the year: Misinformation. Here's why." *Washington Post*. *www.washingtonpost.com/education/2018/12/10/word-year-misinformation-heres-why/*.

Tandoc, Edson C, Zheng Wei Lim and Richard Ling. 2018. "Defining 'fake news': A typology of scholarly definitions." *Digital Journalism* 6(2):137–153.

The Associated Press. 2018. "Florida woman: Airline told me to flush pet hamster." *The Associated Press*.

Thorson, Emily. 2016. "Belief echoes: The persistent effects of corrected misinformation." *Political Communication* 33(3):460–480.

Thorson, Emily A. 2018. FOURTEEN comparing approaches to journalistic fact checking. In Brian G. Southwell, Emily A. Thorson, and Laura Sheble (eds.), *Misinformation and mass audiences*. University of Texas Press pp. 249–262.

Toff, Benjamin, Sumitra Badrinathan, Camila Mont'Alverne, et al. 2021. "Listening to what trust in news means to users: qualitative evidence from four countries." Oxford: Reuters Institute for the Study of Journalism. *https://ora.ox.ac.uk/objects/uuid:f11227fa-45fd-48c9-80e5-64807691f80e*.

Tsfati, Yariv, Hajo G. Boomgaarden, Jesper Strömbäck, et al. 2020. "Causes and consequences of mainstream media dissemination of fake news: Literature review and synthesis." *Annals of the International Communication Association* 44(2):157–173.

Monmouth University. 2020. Monmouth University National Poll. Technical report Monmouth University.

Urban, Juliane and Wolfgang Schweiger. 2014. "News quality from the recipients' perspective: Investigating recipients' ability to judge the normative quality of news." *Journalism Studies* 15(6):821–840.

Uscinski, Joseph, Casey Klofstad and Matthew Atkinson. 2016. "What drives conspiratorial beliefs? The role of informational cues and predispositions." *Political Research Quarterly* 69(1):57–71.

Usher, Nikki. 2021. *News for the rich, white, and blue: How place and power distort American journalism*. Columbia University Press.

Vaccari, Cristian and Andrew Chadwick. 2020. "Deepfakes and disinformation: Exploring the impact of synthetic political video on deception, uncertainty, and trust in news." *Social Media+ Society* 6(1):2056305120903408.

van der Meer, Toni GLA, Michael Hameleers and Jakob Ohme. 2023. "Can fighting misinformation have a negative spillover effect? how warnings for the threat of misinformation can decrease general news credibility." *Journalism Studies* 24(6):1–21.

Van Duyn, Emily and Jessica Collier. 2018. "Priming and fake news: The effects of elite discourse on evaluations of news media." *Mass Communication and Society* 22(1):29–48.

Veiga, Christine. 2023. "To build trust in the age of AI, journalists need new standards and disclosures." *Poynter. www.poynter.org/commentary/ 2023/jouranlism-artificial-intelligence-ethical-uses/.*

Von Hohenberg, Bernhard Clemm and Andrew M. Guess. 2022. "When do sources persuade? The effect of source credibility on opinion change." *Journal of Experimental Political Science* 10(3):1–15.

Vraga, Emily K. and Leticia Bode. 2017. "Using expert sources to correct health misinformation in social media." *Science Communication* 39(5):621–645.

Vraga, Emily K. and Leticia Bode. 2020. "Defining misinformation and understanding its bounded nature: Using expertise and evidence for describing misinformation." *Political Communication* 37(1):136–144.

Wahl-Jorgensen, Karin and Matt Carlson. 2021. "Conjecturing fearful futures: Journalistic discourses on deepfakes." *Journalism Practice* 15(6):803–820.

Wardle, Claire. 2018. "5 lessons for reporting in an age of disinformation." *First Draft* 28. *https://firstdraftnews.org/articles/5-lessons-for-reporting-in-an-age-of-disinformation/.*

Wardle, Claire and Hossein Derakhshan. 2017. *Information disorder: Toward an interdisciplinary framework for research and policymaking.* Vol. 27 Council of Europe.

Wells, Chris, Dhavan Shah, Josephine Lukito, et al. 2020. "Trump, Twitter, and news media responsiveness: A media systems approach." *New Media & Society* 22(4):659–682.

Wood, Thomas, & Porter, Ethan. 2019. "The elusive backfire effect: Mass attitudes' steadfast factual adherence." *Political Behavior* 41:135–163.

Young, Dannagal G., Kathleen Hall Jamieson, Shannon Poulsen and Abigail Goldring. 2018. "Fact-checking effectiveness as a function of format and tone: Evaluating FactCheck. org and FlackCheck. org." *Journalism & Mass Communication Quarterly* 95(1):49–75.

Zhang, Yini, Chris Wells, Song Wang and Karl Rohe. 2018. "Attention and amplification in the hybrid media system: The composition and activity of Donald Trump's Twitter following during the 2016 presidential election." *New Media & Society* 20(9):3161–3182.

Cambridge Elements ☰

Politics and Communication

Stuart Soroka
University of California

Stuart Soroka is a Professor in the Department of Communication at the University of California, Los Angeles, and Adjunct Research Professor at the Center for Political Studies at the Institute for Social Research, University of Michigan. His research focuses on political communication, political psychology, and the relationships between public policy, public opinion, and mass media. His books with Cambridge University Press include The Increasing Viability of Good News (2021, with Yanna Krupnikov), Negativity in Democratic Politics (2014), Information and Democracy (forthcoming, with Christopher Wlezien) and Degrees of Democracy (2010, with Christopher Wlezien).

About the series

Cambridge Elements in Politics and Communication publishes research focused on the intersection of media, technology, and politics. The series emphasizes forward-looking reviews of the field, path-breaking theoretical and methodological innovations, and the timely application of social-scientific theory and methods to current developments in politics and communication around the world.

Cambridge Elements $^{\equiv}$

Politics and Communication

Elements in the series

Home Style Opinion
Joshua P. Darr, Matthew P. Hitt, Johanna L. Dunaway

Power in Ideas
Kirsten Adams, Daniel Kreiss

Economic News
Rens Vliegenthart, Alyt Damstra, Mark Boukes, Jeroen Jonkman

The Increasing Viability of Good News
Stuart Soroka, Yanna Krupnikov

Digital Transformations of the Public Arena
Andreas Jungherr, Ralph Schroeder

Battleground
Lewis A. Friedland, Dhavan V. Shah, Michael W. Wagner, Katherine J. Cramer,
Chris Wells, Jon Pevehouse

Constructing Political Expertise in the News
Kathleen Searles, Yanna Krupnikov, John Barry Ryan, Hillary Style

The YouTube Apparatus
Kevin Munger

How News Coverage of Misinformation Shapes Perceptions and Trust
Emily Thorson

A full series listing is available at: www.cambridge.org/EPCM

Printed in the United States
by Baker & Taylor Publisher Services